BERLIOZ: *SYMPHONIE FANTASTIQUE*

Berlioz's *Symphonie Fantastique* is a key work in the understanding of romanticism, programme music, and the development of the orchestra post-Beethoven. It is noted for having a title and a detailed programme, and for its connection with the composer's personal life and loves. This handbook situates the symphony within its time, and considers influences, literary as well as musical, that shaped its conception. Providing a close analysis of the symphony, its formal properties and melodic and textural elements (including harmony and counterpoint), it is a rich but accessible study which will appeal to music lovers, scholars, and students. It contains a translation of the programme, which sheds light on the form and character of each movement, and the unusual use of a melodic *idée fixe* representing a beloved woman. The unusual five-movement design permits a range of musical topics to be discussed and related to traditional symphonic elements: sonata form, a long adagio, dance-type movements, and thematic development.

JULIAN RUSHTON is Emeritus Professor, School of Music, University of Leeds. His publications include *The Musical Language of Berlioz* (1983), *The Music of Berlioz* (2001), and as editor, *The Cambridge Berlioz Encyclopedia* (2018). He is past president of the Royal Musical Association and an honorary member of the American Musicological Society.

T0334705

NEW CAMBRIDGE MUSIC HANDBOOKS

Series Editor

NICOLE GRIMES, UNIVERSITY OF CALIFORNIA, IRVINE

The New Cambridge Music Handbooks series provides accessible introductions to landmarks in music history, written by leading experts in their field. Encompassing a wide range of musical styles and genres, it embraces the music of hitherto under-represented creators as well as re-imagining works from the established canon. It will enrich the musical experience of students, scholars, listeners and performers alike.

Books in the Series

Hensel: String Quartet in E flat
Benedict Taylor

Berlioz: Symphonie Fantastique
Julian Rushton

Margaret Bonds: The Montgomery Variations and Du Bois 'Credo'
John Michael Cooper

Schoenberg: 'Night Music', Verklärte Nacht and Erwartung
Arnold Whittall

Forthcoming Titles

Schubert: The 'Great' Symphony in C major
Suzannah Clark

Bach: The Cello Suites
Edward Klorman

Clara Schumann: Piano Concerto in A minor Op. 7
Julie Pedneault-Deslauriers

Donizetti: Lucia di Lammermoor
Mark Pottinger

Beethoven: String Quartet Op. 130
Elaine Sisman

Louise Farrenc: Nonet for Winds and Strings
Marie Sumner Lott

Cavalleria rusticana *and* Pagliacci
Alexandra Wilson

BERLIOZ: *SYMPHONIE FANTASTIQUE*

JULIAN RUSHTON
University of Leeds

CAMBRIDGE
UNIVERSITY PRESS

Shaftesbury Road, Cambridge CB2 8EA, United Kingdom

One Liberty Plaza, 20th Floor, New York, NY 10006, USA

477 Williamstown Road, Port Melbourne, VIC 3207, Australia

314–321, 3rd Floor, Plot 3, Splendor Forum, Jasola District Centre,
New Delhi – 110025, India

103 Penang Road, #05–06/07, Visioncrest Commercial, Singapore 238467

Cambridge University Press is part of Cambridge University Press & Assessment,
a department of the University of Cambridge.

We share the University's mission to contribute to society through the pursuit of
education, learning and research at the highest international levels of excellence.

www.cambridge.org
Information on this title: www.cambridge.org/9781316513835

DOI: 10.1017/9781009075138

First published 2024

A catalogue record for this publication is available from the British Library.

Library of Congress Cataloging-in-Publication Data
NAMES: Rushton, Julian, author.
TITLE: Berlioz: symphonie fantastique / Julian Rushton.
Other titles: Symphonie fantastique
DESCRIPTION: [First edition]. | Cambridge, United Kingdom ; New York, NY :
Cambridge University Press, 2023. | Series: New Cambridge music handbooks |
Includes bibliographical references and index.
IDENTIFIERS: LCCN 2023023916 (print) | LCCN 2023023917 (ebook) | ISBN
9781316513835 (hardback) | ISBN 9781009074889 (paperback) | ISBN
9781009075138 (ebook)
SUBJECTS: LCSH: Berlioz, Hector, 1803–1869. Symphonie fantastique. | Berlioz,
Hector, 1803–1869 – Influence. | Symphonies – Analysis, appreciation.
CLASSIFICATION: LCC MT130.B48 R8 2023 (print) | LCC MT130.B48 (ebook) | DDC
784.18/4–dc23/eng/20230531
LC record available at https://lccn.loc.gov/2023023916
LC ebook record available at https://lccn.loc.gov/2023023917

ISBN 978-1-316-51383-5 Hardback
ISBN 978-1-009-07488-9 Paperback

To David Cairns, with admiration and affection

CONTENTS

ILLUSTRATIONS AND BOX

Illustrations

Box

viii

TABLES

MUSIC EXAMPLES

PREFACE AND ACKNOWLEDGEMENTS

Berlioz's *Episode in the Life of an Artist*, now routinely referred to in English as the *Fantastic Symphony*, is 'programme music', a wide-ranging term embracing musical works with titles that are not simply generic.[1] We do not refer to it as 'Berlioz's Symphony No. 1'. Several earlier symphonies were given titles by their composers, and some have nicknames acquired later, such as Mozart's last symphony ('Jupiter'). Berlioz probably knew little of eighteenth-century precedents, but he knew Beethoven's titled third (*Eroica*) and sixth (*Pastoral*) symphonies (see Chapter 3). However, symphonies with evocative titles were uncommon before the nineteenth century; indeed before 1830 when *Symphonie fantastique* was first performed.

The existence of titles and programmes bears on the eternal and possibly insoluble question of musical meaning. Music is often functional, used for dancing or other kinds of entertainment; music attached to words supports, or should support, the lyric or dramatic texts. But can music convey meaning, or some other kind of message, on its own? Early in the nineteenth century writers such as E.T.A. Hoffmann, himself a composer, were beginning to interpret even untitled works, like Beethoven's Fifth Symphony, in terms that suggested profound significance of a kind that could not adequately be expressed in words; for Hoffmann, music was the most romantic of the arts precisely because it reached beyond the events of life or, transcending them, reached the numinous or sublime.[2]

A growing tendency to compose instrumental music with a title and an implied or explicit programme received a major stimulus from Berlioz's work. It preceded by nearly a quarter-century the coinage of the term 'symphonic poem' associated with Franz Liszt, who had previously played a significant part in the early history of *Symphonie fantastique*. But symphonic poems are usually single-movement affairs, their direct ancestor being the titled concert overture. Some of these, such as Beethoven's *Coriolan*, live mainly in the concert hall despite being commissioned to preface a drama, but other overtures, like numerous piano 'preludes', were composed as short instrumental works not intended to precede a drama, though they might refer to one, for instance Mendelssohn's *Midsummer Night's Dream*, composed long before his incidental music to the play, or they may be picturesque, like his *Hebrides* overture. Berlioz had himself composed two overtures before embarking on his first symphony. One, for an opera that was never staged, *Les Francs-juges*, has survived in the concert hall; the other, *Waverley*, the first of his five concert overtures, is prefaced with a quotation from the eponymous novel (1814) by Walter Scott.

At about fifty-five minutes, *Symphonie fantastique* is a long symphony for its time, as were some of Beethoven's. Whatever was new about the work, it was not that it had a title, and was orchestral music associated with a narrative. What marks it as exceptional is the detailed story supplied by the composer; and that the story, unlike the titled overtures mentioned, is the composer's own. This is sometimes misunderstood. The programme is not strictly autobiographical; almost none of the events described actually happened. But it is no one else's story, and Berlioz intended the audience to listen with his complete, strangely dreamlike narrative in mind.

Symphonie fantastique, composed in late 1829 and early 1830 at the cusp of Berlioz's artistic maturity, was written under considerable stress involving his love life, finances, and career prospects. The composer is lightly disguised as the 'artist' of the programme. Berlioz's later works refer to pre-existing literature, for instance those based on Shakespeare's *The Tempest* (late 1830), *King Lear* (1831), and *Romeo and Juliet* (1839). But the narrative of *Symphonie fantastique* was itself a new creation, taking programme music along a new path. The programme reflects Berlioz's inner feelings – although not, fortunately, his real-life actions.

Chapter 1 includes a translation of the programme, following consideration of Berlioz's life in the years preceding his decision to compose the work, and concludes with an outline of the whole symphony, a framework for later discussion of each movement in turn (Chapters 4–8). Even such a strikingly original piece of music is not created in isolation, so the next chapters consider the historical and cultural contexts within which Berlioz lived and worked. Chapter 2 connects him to the burgeoning of French romanticism, and reviews aspects of his musical education, set in relief by comparison with a symphony composed at the same time by his younger colleague Felix Mendelssohn. Chapter 3 considers the major literary and musical influences that most affected Berlioz up to the symphony's composition and premiere.

Chapters 4–8 discuss each movement in terms of musical form, thematically and harmonically defined, exemplifying details of particular interest or originality and mentioning the revisions made before its definitive version, represented by the full score, published as late as 1845. The remaining chapters suggest ways in which this remarkable composition was received; first in Chapter 9 by Berlioz himself, leading to his producing a sequel (*Lélio, or the Return to Life*), then by other composers. Chapter 10 engages with one of the symphony's more controversial aspects, at least for music theory and analysis: the debate on Berlioz's use, or abuse, of sonata form, a debate initiated by another composer, Robert Schumann. Other angles of approach, both to the music and the programme, are considered here and in the final chapter.

***

Since the 1830s critics, musicologists, analysts, and annotators of concert programmes and recordings have written a great deal about *Symphonie fantastique*, often with insight. I cannot claim to have read everything, and I have not added much from authors already mentioned in my earlier books. I have tried to take account of published work more recent than *The Music of Berlioz* (2001) which, like *The Musical Language of Berlioz* (1983), has several pages on *Symphonie fantastique*. The Select Bibliography includes works in English – and other languages – that are worth exploring, including some not actually mentioned in the text.

My feelings about the symphony have not fundamentally altered since 2001, but I have tried to gather thoughts that go back further, and to view it from different angles. My interest in it started when my undergraduate supervisor, Raymond Leppard, suggested I write an essay on 'Berlioz's attitude to symphonic form'. This encouraged me to buy miniature scores, which I took to the Edinburgh Festival in the 1960s; there I heard *Symphonie fantastique* with its sequel, *Lélio*, under Colin Davis, the first conductor to record nearly all of Berlioz's output.

Immediately after another Edinburgh performance I came across Berlioz's future biographer David Cairns, with smoke (almost) coming from his nostrils: 'That man's never seen a metronome in his life!' he said to anyone within earshot (the conductor, Lorin Maazel, had exceeded the speed limit in the finale). All of us interested in Berlioz are eternally indebted to David, and I acknowledge with gratitude the work of many other Berlioz scholars mentioned within. I also warmly acknowledge the support of these, and more, over the years, particularly Hugh Macdonald for his encouragement in the early stages of my developing interest in this composer, and for inviting me to edit some volumes in the New Berlioz Edition, of which he is General Editor. My thanks go also to Cambridge University Press, to the series editor Nicole Grimes, to the excellent copy-editor Frances Tye, and to the anonymous reader of the first – which I rashly hoped would be the final – draft of the text.

In 2019 the 150th anniversary of Berlioz's death was commemorated by the launch of 'Berlioz 150' by Lord Aberdare (Chairman of the Berlioz Society). This has produced 'Fantastique for Schools', an educational programme which, it is to be hoped, will continue to inspire younger listeners to explore music simplistically labelled 'classical' (and all too often considered 'elitist'). Berlioz was a major player in the subset of such music generally called 'romantic', and has been perceived, from a perspective that views the mainstream as Austrian and German, as an outsider. But his work is in a kind of dialogue with these and other predecessors, in which respect he was very much an artist of his time. His music, not only *Symphonie fantastique*, has achieved wider-than-ever acceptance and prominence since 1969, the centenary of his death, and he continues to interest fellow composers up to the present day. His place in the pantheon of significant and pioneering European composers, often disputed, is by now secure.

Notes

1. See, for instance, Jonathan Kregor, *Program Music* (Cambridge Introductions to Music, Cambridge: Cambridge University Press, 2015).
2. E.T.A. Hoffmann, *Review of Beethoven's Fifth Symphony, Allgemeine Musikalische Zeitung* xii (July 1810). Translations in Elliot Forbes (ed.), *Beethoven. Symphony No. 5 in C Minor*, Norton Critical Score (London: Chappell & Co., 1971), 150–63, and David Charlton (ed.), *E. T. A. Hoffmann's Musical Writings*, trans. Martyn Clarke (Cambridge: Cambridge University Press, 1989), 234–51.

ABBREVIATIONS

Citations in the notes after the first reference take the form: author, short title, page. Full details are also in the bibliography. The following abbreviations are used for items frequently referenced, and are listed here as a memorandum, although a full reference is given at the first mention in the notes, and in the bibliography. All unattributed translations are by the author.

Works by Berlioz

Berlioz's *Memoirs*:	References to whole chapters without qualification refer to a relatively extended passage which can be consulted in any edition.
	Chapter numbers are those of the original edition and correspond to the most recent editions in French and English:
Mémoires (ed. Bloom):	*Mémoires d'Hector Berlioz de 1803 à 1865.* Text prepared, introduced and annotated by Peter Bloom (Paris: Vrin, 2019).
The Memoirs (trans. Cairns):	*The Memoirs of Hector Berlioz.* Translated and edited by David Cairns, revised second edition (London: Allen Lane/The Penguin Press, 2002).
Cone, *Fantastic Symphony*:	Edward T. Cone, *Berlioz: Fantastic Symphony*, Norton

	Critical Score (London: Chappell, 1971).
NBE:	New Berlioz Edition (General Editor Hugh Macdonald), 26 vols. (Kassel: Bärenreiter, 1967–2005).
NBE 16:	Berlioz, *Symphonie fantastique* (ed. Nicholas Timperley), New Berlioz Edition vol. 16 (1972).

Alphabetical Abbreviations Used in the Notes:

CBE:	Julian Rushton (ed.), *The Cambridge Berlioz Encyclopedia* (Cambridge: Cambridge University Press, 2018)
CG (plus volume number):	Hector Berlioz, *Correspondance générale*, Vols. I–VIII (Paris: Flammarion, 1972); Vol. IX (Paris: Actes Sud, 2016)

INTRODUCTION, PROGRAMME, OUTLINE

The full title of Berlioz's first symphony is *Épisode de la vie d'un artiste. Symphonie fantastique en cinq parties* (Episode in an artist's life: Fantastic Symphony in five movements). It was completed in April 1830 and its programme was published in *Le Figaro* on 21 May. However, the rehearsal on 16 May went so badly that the intended premiere was cancelled; the first performance eventually took place on 5 December, shortly before the composer's twenty-seventh birthday. Although the symphony soon became, and remains, one of Berlioz's best-known works, its second performance was not until two years later, almost to the day.

As the symphony was nearing completion in February 1830, Berlioz described his emotional state in a letter to his father, who was a doctor; one can read into it an understanding of his own creative fever and the need to suppress it in order carry on working. His account of a severe toothache modulates into a frank comment on self-absorption, mingling present events with past memories:

I have adopted the habit of observing myself all the time, so no sensation escapes me, and reflection doubles it; I see myself as if in a mirror. I experience extraordinary feelings of which I can hardly give an idea, seemingly caused by nervous exaltation, which resembles intoxication with opium. What surprises me is that I well remember feeling just the same way at the age of twelve[.][1]

Letters of this period to his close friends the poet Humbert Ferrand and the pianist and composer Ferdinand Hiller are more open about the anguish he suffered from unrequited love and unfounded rumours about the behaviour of the object of his passion, the Irish actress Harriet Smithson, whom he had not even met. These feelings are implicit in the programme of the symphony, which, in turn, may have had a therapeutic effect; its completion should have served to restore his self-confidence. He managed to turn the rehearsal debacle in May to advantage by making revisions; and between May and December 1830, his life changed fundamentally. On the rebound from Harriet Smithson's refusal to meet him, he became engaged to be married to the pianist Camille Moke; and at the fifth attempt, he won the prestigious Prix de Rome (Rome Prize) awarded to artists and musicians by the Académie des Beaux-Arts.[2]

The Prix de Rome

During the hottest days of July 1830, Berlioz was immured in the Institut de France, one of six aspiring composers all setting the same text, a dramatic cantata, *La Mort de Sardanapale*. At the same time the 'July Revolution' broke out and overthrew the last Bourbon king, Charles X, an event which has been seen as a political parallel to the cultural stirrings that led in due course to romanticism's becoming established as a leading artistic tendency, displacing the stuffy neoclassicism associated with the *ancien régime*: 'By 1850 ... the superiority of inspiration, emotion, and subjective judgment over tradition, rules, and skill was now official.'[3] This comment refers to sculpture, where, as with music, skills cannot be dispensed with, for they are as essential in preparing works of romantic inspiration and subjectivity as they are for works that maintain tradition and adhere to the rules, or are purely decorative. It is the rules that mostly explain Berlioz's four earlier failures in the Prix de Rome, for he often broke them; his rivals behaved better, but none established a reputation comparable to his, and all are now practically unknown.

From early 1831, Berlioz was based at the French Academy in Rome (the Villa Medici). While there he made further revisions to *Symphonie fantastique* and assembled its sequel ('complément') in the form of a monodrama ('mélologue'), mixing music and speech. The programme includes the imaginary death of the protagonist, so the sequel was poignantly entitled *Le Retour à la vie* (The Return to Life); it is usually known by its later title, *Lélio, ou le Retour à la vie*, or simply *Lélio* (see Chapter 9).

Berlioz did not want to leave Paris, and by 1830 he had a considerable if disputed reputation on which to build. But he competed for the prize not only for the income it provided but from a need to mollify his father, who disapproved of his musical ambitions and periodically withdrew financial support. In 1826 he failed the preliminary test in fugue. He then enrolled in the Paris Conservatoire class of Antoine Reicha, and in each of the four following years he passed the preliminary test and entered the Institut to compose a cantata. In 1827 his *La Mort d'Orphée* was declared 'unplayable' at the trial performance because the rehearsal pianist was unable to play it; that it was written for orchestra was not considered relevant. In 1828 *Herminie* was awarded second prize. In the previous three years the 'Deuxième Grand Prix' had been awarded first prize the following year, as if by right, and this encouraged Berlioz to take risks in 1829 with his *La Mort de Cléopâtre*. In the interests of expressive realism he violated not only rules but the judges' perception of good taste; some of them found his music unpardonable. No first prize was awarded that year. In 1830 Berlioz took care to write down to the level of his judges. Nevertheless, he conducted a performance of *La Mort de Sardanapale* after returning from Rome, before abandoning this cantata, of which only a fragment survives.

Berlioz habitually recycled good ideas from abandoned works, as did many composers, including his first musical hero, Christoph Willibald Gluck (1714–87). Berlioz was self-critical, and destroyed much of his early music once he had exhausted its usefulness. Autographs of the 1828 and 1829 cantatas were preserved in the Institut archives, and when *Herminie* was unearthed it was found to contain the principal theme of *Symphonie fantastique*, identified in the programme as the *idée fixe* (see Chapter 4).[4] It does not necessarily follow that the melody was inspired by the emotions of the cantata's protagonist; he could have thought of it earlier and carried it in his head in case it proved useful when composing under prison-like conditions.

Out of sympathy with Italian musical culture, Berlioz found it hard to work in Rome, but before returning to Paris he wrote the words of *Lélio* and assembled its music from existing works. These include his Shakespearean fantasy, *La Tempête*, composed after *Symphonie fantastique* but performed first (7 November 1830). In 1831, temporarily away from Rome, he composed two overtures inspired by literature: *Le Roi Lear* after Shakespeare and *Rob-Roy* after Walter Scott. Required to send sacred music to Paris as a condition of the Rome Prize and as evidence of diligence and progress, he cheekily sent a copy of the 'Resurrexit' from his *Messe solennelle* of 1824, although it had been performed in Paris five times (most recently in 1829). It was not recognized, and the Academy's report praised Berlioz for restraining his over-active imagination, a barb perhaps aimed at the 1829 cantata *Cléopâtre* but certainly at *Symphonie fantastique*.[5]

'Stella montis'

The opening melody of *Symphonie fantastique* originated much earlier, during Berlioz's semi-rural youth in La Côte-Saint-André, Isère, in south-eastern France. Hector was the eldest of six children, all of whom predeceased him; only two sisters had survived into adulthood.[6] He was expected to inherit his father's respectable position in the local community, and was sent to Paris shortly before his eighteenth birthday to study medicine. Hearing music professionally performed for the first time, including operas, hardened his resolution to defy his parents and become a musician.

The symphony's opening Largo harks back to an early love. Berlioz said his youthful songs were melancholy and in minor keys, but all that survive, including his earliest published works composed as a teenager, are in major keys. Just one, that was not published and is lost, is known to have been in a minor key. It set a poem from *Estelle et Némorin*, the novel by Jean-Pierre-Claris de Florian (1755–94) which Berlioz read and reread as a boy. The tune 'presented itself humbly to my mind when I began to write my Fantastic Symphony in 1829. It seemed to me suited to express the overpowering sadness of a young heart first tortured by a hopeless love, and I welcomed it'.[7]

Florian's heroine shared the forename of a real person who lived near Berlioz's grandfather, whom he often visited in Meylan, near Grenoble.[8] Aged twelve, he fell head over heels in love with Estelle Dubœuf, then eighteen. Their age difference made even

4

friendship impossible, but she became his ideal, his 'Stella montis' (mountain star) and he was unkindly mocked for his passion, even by his mother. In the 1860s he reintroduced himself to her (she was now Madame Fornier, and a widow); their brief friendship led him, when rewriting his will in 1867 after the death of his son Louis, to offer her an annuity: 'I beg her to accept this modest sum as a memento of the sentiments that I have harboured for her *throughout my lifetime*' (she accepted). The song was probably composed not long before the seventeen-year-old Berlioz left for Paris. The first lines suggest what he may have been feeling:

> Je vais donc quitter pour jamais
> Mon doux pays, ma douce amie,
> Loin d'eux je vais traîner ma vie
> Dans les pleurs et dans les regrets!

'I must leave my dear homeland forever, and my sweet love; far away, I shall drag out my life in tears and regrets!' Florian's poem can be fitted to the tune up to a point. It was probably not in the same key as the symphony, and the original accompaniment – perhaps for guitar, which Berlioz played well – must have been entirely different.[9] In Berlioz's most ambitious early song, *Le Montagnard exilé* (published by early 1823), the mountaineer sings of his sorrow, exiled from the 'paternal roof' and its associations; the poem by Berlioz's friend Albert du Boys mentions the Isère, the river that gives its name to their home region. Berlioz's adolescent turmoil contributed to a sensation reflected in the symphony's programme, an extreme reaction to loneliness ('isolement'):

From the age of sixteen, he suffered from what he called *mal de l'isolement*, a problem at once mental, nervous, and imaginary whose symptoms included intense longing, 'a feeling of loneliness and absence', and a sense of terrible constriction.[10]

He described the condition in connection with his Italian exile: 'A vacuum forms round my panting chest, and it is as if my heart, subject to an irresistible force of suction, were evaporating and about to dissolve. The skin smarts and burns.'[11] He called the condition 'spleen', distinguishing active and passive forms; active spleen embraces life and happiness, but passive spleen is world-weary: life seems to have no meaning. From an artistic viewpoint, what matters is the force of these sensations, and their coexistence within him; their musical analogue is found in much of his work, including the third movement of *Symphonie fantastique*.

Berlioz's earliest *mal de l'isolement* derived from family conflicts, when even his sisters refused to take seriously his dreams of music and love for 'Stella montis'. He had later loves, notably Harriet Smithson and his second wife, Marie Recio, as well as women friends and confidantes, but 'Stella' lies behind elements in *Symphonie fantastique* that suggest nostalgia – which, if truly a 'Swiss disease', originated not far from Estelle's home in Meylan; from there, the Alps are visible in the east.

The Programme of *Symphonie fantastique*

On 16 April 1830, Berlioz confided to Humbert Ferrand (also his literary collaborator in the 1820s) that he was completing a 'grande symphonie fantastique', adding a preliminary version of its programme, not much different from what would be offered to audiences in December. He sets out the ideas behind its five movements:

Part I: double, made up of a short adagio, followed at once by an extended allegro (flux of passions; pointless reveries; delirious passion with every element of tenderness, jealousy, rage, fears, etc. etc.)

Part II: Scene in the country (adagio, thoughts of love and hope troubled by dark foreboding).

Part III: A ball (brilliant and intoxicating music).

Part IV: March to Execution (ferocious, pompous music).

Part V: Dream of a Sabbath night.

In the letter he expanded this in detail, with an introductory paragraph almost identical to what was printed for the first performance.[12]

The main difference between this outline and the final version is the order of the second and third movements. Berlioz soon decided that the foreboding that disrupts the country scene should lead to a crisis of despair, when the protagonist tries to poison himself; the last two movements are a nightmare induced by the poison. Berlioz reconsidered the programme when the symphony and *Lélio* were performed together in Weimar in 1855. He now decided that the whole symphony should be considered a series of increasingly terrifying dreams. My translation follows, based on the text in the published full score (1845); the many variants, all small other than those mentioned, are detailed in the New Berlioz Edition (NBE).[13]

Box 1.1: Programme

The composer aims to develop, as far as is musically possible, some aspects of an artist's life. The plan of this instrumental drama, unaided by words, requires prior explanation. This programme should be considered equivalent to spoken dialogue in opera, introducing and motivating the character and expression of each musical movement.*

* Making the programme available to audiences at concerts including this symphony is indispensable to full understanding of the work [Berlioz's note].

Part One: Rêveries, Passions (Day-Dreams, Suffering)

I suggest that a young musician, affected by the mental complaint a celebrated author [Chateaubriand] has termed *flux of passions* [*vague des passions*], sees for the first time a woman with the perfect charm conjured in his dreams, and falls hopelessly in love. By a freakish accident, her image only comes to mind combined with a musical idea, which seems to have the character – passionate, but also noble and reticent – he attributes to his beloved.

This imagined image and its musical parallel haunt him unceasingly like a double *idée fixe*. This explains the return in each of the symphony's movements of the melody that begins the first Allegro. Hence the first movement passes from a state of melancholy reverie, interrupted by bursts of unfounded happiness and stirrings of anger and jealousy, returning to tenderness, tears, and religious consolation.

Part Two: Un Bal (A Dance)

The artist finds himself in diverse situations; in the middle of the *tumult of a ball*, in peaceful contemplation of the beauties of nature. But wherever he goes, in the town or the countryside, the beloved image comes to him and troubles his soul.

Box 1.1: (*cont.*)

Part Three: Scène aux champs (Country Scene)
Finding himself one evening in the fields, he hears in the distance two peasants exchanging cow-calls [*ranz des vaches*]; their pastoral dialogue, the rural scene, the leaves gently whispering in the breeze, all contribute to a new hopefulness, encouraging a strange calm and lending his thoughts a brighter colour. He contemplates his loneliness; he hopes it will soon be over ... But if she were to deceive him! ... This blend of hope and fear, possible happiness disturbed by dark foreboding, forms the topic of the Adagio. Finally, one peasant resumes the *ranz des vaches*; there is no reply ... Distant rumbling of thunder ... solitude ... silence ...

Part IV 'Marche au supplice' (March to Execution)
Now sure he loves in vain, the artist poisons himself with opium. The dose of the drug, too weak to kill him, induces deep sleep accompanied by nightmares. He dreams he has murdered his beloved; condemned to death, he witnesses *his own execution*. He is led in a procession to sounds of a march, now dark and fierce, now brilliant and grand; the dull funereal tramping leads without transition to the most explosive outbursts. Finally, the first bars of the *idée fixe* are heard, like a last thought of the beloved before the fatal fall of the guillotine.

Part V 'Songe d'une nuit de Sabbat' (Dream of a Witches' Sabbath)
He sees himself at the Sabbath among a dreadful band of ghosts, sorcerers, and all kinds of monsters assembled for his funeral. Weird sounds, groans, shrieks of laughter, are heard in the distance and seemingly answered. The beloved melody reappears, but it has lost its noble and reticent character; it has become a vulgar dance, trivial and grotesque; *she* has come to the Sabbath ... Shouts of delight at her arrival ... She joins the devilish revelry ... Funeral bells, burlesque parody of the *Dies irae*.* *Sabbath round dance* [*Ronde du sabbat*]. The round dance and *Dies irae* combined.
* Hymn sung at Catholic funeral ceremonies [Berlioz's note].

***

The programme offers a way of understanding Berlioz's expressive intentions, but its relationship to the music is not over-literal. He refers to it as equivalent to the spoken dialogue in an *opéra comique*, which motivates, rather than being part of, the music of that genre. In a preview of the performance, François-Joseph Fétis referred to the symphony with programme as a sort of novel ('roman'). This analogy had occurred to Berlioz himself, as he wrote to Ferrand: 'this is how I've woven my novel, or better my story, in which you'll have no difficulty in recognizing the hero'.[14] 'Reveries and passions' run throughout, with the former predominant in the first and third movements. The role of the *idée fixe*, principal theme of the first movement, is explained by the programme for the March and finale, but not for the second and third movements. The 1830 programme shown here says almost nothing about the second movement, but the revised version prepared a quarter-century later reads: 'He meets the beloved at a dance in the midst of the glittering tumult of a party', a meeting that gives rise to hope that his passion might be returned and so induces the initial calm of the third movement. The finale's programme does not suggest that over half its bars come after the burlesque parody. The last words are intended to draw attention to a purely musical feature, a climactic combination of themes such as Berlioz often used in later works.

Peter Bloom found a possible source for the original title and the *idée fixe*:

a certain 'Épisode de la vie d'un voyageur', in which a young man wanders round Paris for a month trying to find the beautiful young woman he has seen but once – a woman whose image appears before his mind's eye, like an *idée fixe*, whenever he sees a rose. The woman meets a tragic fate. Did Berlioz – who tells us of the extraordinary images he saw in his *own* mind's eye – read this book?[15]

The combination of 'Épisode de la vie . . .' and *idée fixe* is certainly striking, although the fate of the woman imagined by Berlioz's programme is undetermined. This book was published in March 1830, so Berlioz could have seen it before he outlined the programme to Ferrand. But it could be a coincidence; Berlioz had decided to write a symphony some months earlier, and by March 1830 it was nearing completion. And there is another possible source for the term *idée fixe*: Francesca Brittan notes its definition in 'French psychiatric ideas of monomania (an unhealthy fixation on a single person, object, or idea), with which Berlioz was clearly familiar'.[16] Literature certainly played its part in the symphony's conception (see Chapter 3). If Berlioz adapted his title from literature, he was not the only composer to do so. Liszt's 'Vallée d'Obermann' (*Années de Pèlerinage* I, 'Suisse') alludes to a semi-autobiographical epistolary novel where the title character is the author's alter ego; Swiss adventures led 'Obermann' to discourse on the *ranz des vaches*. (Did Berlioz read *this* book?)[17]

An Outline of *Symphonie fantastique*

Most earlier symphonies have three or four movements, but an obvious precedent for five is Beethoven's Sixth Symphony (*Pastoral*), with its crisis (thunderstorm) similarly placed as the fourth movement.

One of the most original aspects of *Symphonie fantastique* is its use of melodies previously set to words. The opening is the Florian romance; the *idée fixe* is sung in *Herminie*; the main theme of the third movement comes from the *Messe solennelle*, and the *Dies irae* chant from the Requiem Mass. Countering that vocal tendency are clearly instrumental ideas: secondary material in the first movement, the waltz theme, the *ranz des vaches*, the March, the fugue in the finale.

Chapters 4–8 include 'maps' of each movement, outlining their forms musically; the bar numbers follow those of the New Berlioz Edition (NBE).[18] When a theme begins on an upbeat, the number is the bar of the following first beat. Where keys are indicated, a capital letter means a major key unless qualified as minor. Here is the overall sequence of keys, which is only a little unusual from the point of view of 'classical' precedents:

Movements I–II: C minor (Largo), C major (Allegro). The quiet ending leads easily to the quiet A-minor harmony that opens movement II; A major is then established as the tonic.

Movements II–III: II is in A with an episode in F; F is also the key of III. The note A is common to both tonic chords, but other elements at the junction of movements (texture, dynamics) are dissimilar, marking the change of atmosphere between ballroom and countryside.

Movements III–IV: F and the March key, G minor, are not directly related, but similar dynamic levels and the use of horn and timpani at the junction of movements form an audible connection.

Movements IV–V: IV ends loudly in G major; V begins quietly on a diminished seventh with the same top note (g'''), a tenuous connection. The tonic of V (C) is only established much later.

In one of the most thorough analyses of the work, Edward T. Cone refers to the succession (C–A–F–G minor–C) as 'a clear pattern', but 'exceptional'. In a work in C, one might expect A to be minor and G to be major. Cone notes a symmetry: II starts and IV ends in the opposite mode to what might be expected; A minor (starting II) follows its relative C major (I), and G major (ending IV) is the dominant of C (V).[19] This is well enough if one overlooks applause between movements, quite normal circa 1830 and after, and (which could also happen) the chance that the audience might demand an encore of a movement before going on to the next.

Berlioz probably did not think of these matters when changing the movement order: 'Un Bal' after 'Scène aux champs' would be unexceptional as to key (F to A minor), but A major to the G minor of the March would have been rather abrupt. The change is likely to have had a programmatic motivation. With the final order, the marked discontinuity between II and III (keys A–F; *fortissimo* to unaccompanied cor anglais) makes an effective contrast: a scene in the city, then a pastoral scene. Either ordering makes a contrast between movements III and IV to fit the change, in the 1830 version of the programme, from a waking to a dreaming protagonist. Yet there is little audible link between the two parts of the opium dream (IV–V); a brazen *tutti* is followed by mysterious, indeterminate rhythm and harmony. The order of movements was not affected when Berlioz revised the programme to represent the whole symphony as a dream from which the sequel *Lélio* is a rude awakening.

After the symphony's second performance (9 December 1832), also the premiere of *Lélio*, Berlioz finally met Harriet Smithson, with whom he had fallen in love five years earlier. After a turbulent courtship, they were married the following October.

Notes

1. Letter to Dr Louis Berlioz, 19 February 1830. *Correspondance Générale* (hereafter *CG*), Vol. I, 309–13; cited 310. 'En outre, l'habitude que j'ai prise de m'observer continuellement fait qu'aucune sensation ne m'échappe et la réflexion la rend double, je me vois dans un miroir. J'éprouve souvent des impressions extraordinaires dont rien ne peut donner une idée, vraisemblablement l'exaltation nerveuse en est la cause, cela tient de l'ivresse de l'opium.

Mais ce qui me surprend c'est que je me rappelle fort bien avoir éprouvé exactement la même chose dès l'âge de 12 ans'.

2. On the Prix de Rome, see Julia Lu and Alexandre Dratwicki (eds.), *Le Concours du prix de Rome de musique (1803–1968)* (Lyons: Symétrie: Centre de musique romantique française, 2011).

3. Charles Rosen and Henri Zerner, *Romanticism and Realism: The Mythology of Nineteenth-Century Art* (London: Faber and Faber, 1984), 10.

4. On 'self-borrowing' see *The Cambridge Berlioz Encyclopedia (CBE)*, 43–5; Hugh Macdonald, 'Berlioz's Self-Borrowings', *Proceedings of the Royal Musical Association* 92 (1965–6): 27–44.

5. Berlioz, *Mémoires*, chap. 39. The Academy's report is quoted in *Mémoires d'Hector Berlioz de 1803 à 1869*, ed. Peter Bloom (Paris: Vrin, 2019), 365.

6. See David Cairns, 'The Berlioz Family', *CBE*, 31–3, and 'Two Sisters' in Cairns, *Discovering Berlioz* (London: Toccata Press, 2019), 91–104.

7. *Memoirs*, chap. 4. David Cairns (trans.), *The Memoirs of Hector Berlioz*, 2nd revised edition (New York: Knopf, 2002), 16; *Mémoires* (ed. Bloom), 146.

8. *Memoirs*, chap. 3. Pascal Beyls, *Estelle Fornier, premier et dernier amour de Berlioz* (Grenoble: Pascal Beyls, 2003).

9. See Julian Rushton, *The Music of Berlioz* (Oxford: Oxford University Press, 2001), 168; Hector Berlioz, *Symphonie fantastique*, ed. Nicholas Temperley (Kassel: Bärenreiter, 1972), New Berlioz Edition (NBE), Vol. 16, 194.

10. Francesca Brittan, 'Health', *CBE*, 158–9. See also Susan Ironfield, 'Creative Developments of the "Mal de l'Isolement" in Berlioz', *Music & Letters*, 59 (1978): 33–48.

11. 'Le vide se fait autour de ma poitrine palpitante, et il semble alors que mon cœur, sous l'aspiration d'une force irrésistible, s'évapore et tend à se dissoudre par expansion. Puis, la peau de tout mon corps devient douloureuse et brûlante'. *The Memoirs* (trans. Cairns), 175–6; *Mémoires* (ed. Bloom), 372.

12. *CG* Vol. I, 319–20; most of the letter is translated in David Cairns, *Berlioz*, Vol. I, *The Making of an Artist* (London: Allen Lane/The Penguin Press), 1999), 359–60.

13. NBE 16, 167–9; the revised programme, 170.

14. '... une sorte de roman'. François-Joseph Fétis, 'Nouvelles de Paris', *La Revue musicale* X (December 1830), 89–90. Berlioz's letter of 16 April 1830: 'voici comment j'ai tissé mon roman, ou plutôt mon histoire, dont il ne vous est pas difficile de reconnaître le héros'. *CG* Vol. I, 319.

15. Peter Bloom, 'Berlioz in the Year of the *Symphonie fantastique*', in *Berlioz in Time: From Early Recognition to Lasting Renown*, Eastman Studies in Music (Rochester, NY: Rochester University Press, 2022), 1–25; cited, 2. Marquis Louis-Rainier Lanfranchi (pseudonym of Étienne-Léon de Lamothe-Langon), *Voyage à Paris ou Esquisses des hommes et des choses de cette capitale* (Paris: Le Petit, 1830), 207–24. My thanks to Peter Bloom for clarifying the month of publication (personal communication).

16. Francesca Brittan, 'Health', *CBE*, 158.

17. Étienne-Jean-Baptise-Pierre-Ignace Pivert de Senancour, *Obermann* (1804) (*Oberman* in some editions).

18. NBE 16 is available as a miniature score (Schott: Edition Eulenburg 422).

19. Edward T. Cone, 'Schumann Amplified', in Cone, *Berlioz: Fantastic Symphony*, Norton Critical Scores (London: Chappell, 1971), 249–77; cited 249–50.

LITERARY AND MUSICAL ROMANTICISM

The poet and novelist Théophile Gautier (1811–72) named three of his older contemporaries as the 'Trinity of French Romanticism': in painting Eugène Delacroix (1798–1863), in literature Victor Hugo (1802–85), and in music Hector Berlioz (1803–69).[1] By 1830, the year of the 'July Revolution', the older pair were already well known. The preface to Hugo's drama *Cromwell* (1827) was a manifesto of romanticism, claiming for the arts elements which academicians and neoclassical playwrights considered to be in poor taste, and barbarous: open forms (influenced by Shakespeare), naturalism, the sublime, and the grotesque. Delacroix exhibited in the 'salon' as early as 1822; his *Death of Sardanapalus* (1827), after Lord Byron's grandly fustian tragedy, was also the subject of Berlioz's 1830 cantata.

Byron's death in the Greek struggle for independence contributed to his romantic aura and inspired Berlioz's early *Scène héroïque* (*La Révolution grecque*, 1825–6), but the composer, still nominally a student, had yet to gain a reputation equal to that of Hugo or Delacroix. That changed in 1830, when works by each of the 'trinity' reshaped the artistic landscape. Hugo's tragedy *Hernani* was staged in February. Its subject and versification challenged conventions of the state theatre, the Comédie française, and led to fighting between adherents of neoclassicism and romanticism, with Gautier in a red waistcoat conspicuous among Hugo's supporters. After the revolution Delacroix stormed artistic barricades with *Liberty Leading the People*, which has been described as 'the apotheosis of the modern banal-heroic'.[2] The phrase, not intended to be derogatory, might fit some of Berlioz's music, such as the finale to *Symphonie funèbre et triomphale* (1840).

When *Symphonie fantastique* was performed, it gained notoriety as well as applause and could hardly be ignored even by the academic establishment. Berlioz had recently published two collections of songs and choruses: in 1829 *Huit Scènes de Faust* (with orchestra) after Goethe, and early in 1830 *Neuf Mélodies irlandaises* (with piano accompaniment), after poems by Byron's friend Thomas Moore (*Irish Melodies*). Berlioz withdrew the *Huit Scènes*, recycling the music in *La Damnation de Faust* (1846), a work he originally referred to as a 'concert opera'. The Irish songs sold better and reappeared in revised editions. But published compositions made little money; the best income from composing would have been a successful opera, and *Les Francs-juges* was rejected on the basis of Ferrand's libretto in 1829. Another possibility to which many composers have resorted to supplement their income is conducting. This was important to Berlioz who, although he sang and played flute, guitar, and percussion to a decent standard, was no virtuoso in the age of Niccolò Paganini, Clara Schumann, and Franz Liszt. Instead he became a virtuoso of the orchestra, the instrument of his major works. But his important conducting career began a few years later; his concerts up to 1834 were mostly directed by others.

Aesthetics

By 1830, Berlioz was already writing occasionally for journals. Until 1863 his most reliable income was from music criticism, and his reviews – mostly constructive, with plenty of good advice to young performers – were seasoned with entertaining diversions, even fiction. He also used his position as a regular contributor to journals to publish a first version of his orchestration treatise, and various meditations on the aesthetics of music. In 1830 he published a manifesto, 'Reflections on classic and romantic music'.[3] His early admiration for Gluck's French operas never waned; these are essentially neoclassical in form and subject matter, but Berlioz found romantic elements in them, and proclaimed Gluck 'the Shakespeare of music'. Fifty years earlier that would have been insulting; Gluck was compared to Shakespeare by those who considered the latter barbarous, and higher praise, as 'the Racine of music', was bestowed on Gluck's rival Niccolò Piccinni.[4] But by 1830, Racine, though still esteemed, was not imitated, for Shakespeare had won over the French romantics.

In his youth, Berlioz's extensive reading included Latin and French classics (Virgil, Racine, La Fontaine) as well as eighteenth-century novels of sentiment by Florian and by Bernardin de Saint-Pierre (*Paul et Virginie*). Following the successive artistic revelations discussed later in this book (Chapter 3) he declared that instrumental music was not mere entertainment, but an independently expressive medium. The language of music, without words, gains strength and freedom from being indeterminate, even 'vague'. Though probably unaware of them, Berlioz might have endorsed the similar claims of the jurist, short-story writer, and critic E. T. A. Hoffmann in his remarkable review of Beethoven's Fifth Symphony.[5] In 1839 Berlioz matched Hoffmann's ideas of the sublime in the preface to the printed libretto of his *Roméo et Juliette* (1839), justifying its mingling of vocal with purely instrumental sections, notably the Adagio of the love scene; in the latter, as in *Symphonie fantastique*, he let his imagination run free, unhampered by the distraction of voices and sung words.

Nevertheless, *Symphonie fantastique* is not exactly wordless. It has its programme – to which Hoffmann among others might well have taken exception. Berlioz may have felt that his music had to be reconciled with the listening habits of a public that adored Rossini, a composer the young Berlioz, in his ardent partisanship for Gluck, affected to despise (he later modified this view). He probably concluded that it would assist understanding of such a 'fantastic' symphony if there were guidance as to the composer's intentions. The programme should liberate rather than restrain the listener's imagination, but he did not think that imagination should roam completely free; as Leonard Bernstein suggests, we should listen to much of Berlioz's music on two levels: the sounds of the music itself and the scene or narrative that runs parallel to it.[6]

Berlioz elsewhere offered only titles, as in his overtures and his next symphony *Harold en Italie*, rather than a full programme. Either Berlioz assumed that audiences would know, or at least know of, *King Lear* and Byron's long poem *Childe Harold's Pilgrimage* or he considered that the works inspired by them could survive as 'just music' – a hope he also entertained, with reservations, for *Symphonie fantastique*. *Roméo et Juliette* has a detailed scenario, sung in the Prologue with anticipations of themes from the following movements. Whereas in *Symphonie fantastique* and *Roméo* the works' titles are supported by verbal narratives, in *Grande Ouverture du Roi Lear* we have to work out the connection to the play for ourselves, assisted by references in letters written much later that identify characterizations of Lear and his daughter Cordelia.[7] And in *Harold en Italie* Berlioz drew more on his own experiences than on Byron, and each movement has its own title.

Eighteenth-century audiences are commonly supposed to have attended symphony concerts and operas for entertainment, rather than for edifying or emotional experiences. But Berlioz clearly expected his audience to pay careful attention to what the wordless music *seems to be saying*. This was then a modern expectation, but by 1830 audiences were becoming increasingly aware that their contribution to such events might include being moved, with emotions focused on a protagonist, possibly the artist's alter ego: 'In forms as different as Wordsworth's *Prelude* and Berlioz's *Symphonie fantastique*, the work of art presents itself as autobiography, as fact, as part of nature.'[8]

Mark Evan Bonds has traced the changed perception of artistic creativity from a form of classical rhetoric to a form of autobiography.[9] Scott Burnham observes that 'Beethoven's music has consistently been judged to be expressive of the primary features of the modern Western concept of self.'[10] Berlioz may have understood Beethoven's symphonies as representing the composer's humanity, personality, and innermost feelings. He certainly did not experience them as entertainment, and he was not averse to including quasi-programmatic comments in his own analyses of Beethoven. For instance, evoking two favourite authors, Berlioz explains the contrast of the funeral march and scherzo in the *Eroica* symphony by evoking, for the latter, the funeral games in Homer's *Iliad*; the first movement of Beethoven's Fifth suggested to him the jealous rage of Shakespeare's Othello.[11]

Although *Symphonie fantastique* evidently chimes with a shift in how music can and should be perceived, Berlioz retained much of the previous century's concern for rhetoric: the art of disposing materials, in sound, image, or words, to arouse a sympathetic response. This required hard work. Berlioz felt his emotions deeply, but he claimed that he had only once composed a complete work under their immediate impact: 'Élégie', the last song in his *Mélodies irlandaises*.[12] He might have approved Wordsworth's dictum that poetry is emotion recollected in tranquillity. When composing his five-act opera *Les Troyens* in the 1850s, Berlioz wrote of music's need to be free even when, paradoxically, setting his own libretto; but he recognized the danger of strong personal feelings in creativity: 'One must strive to do the hottest things coldly.'[13]

Engaged in the hard work of creation, artists may feign or remember emotions; they are not directly experienced as they work. Composers need not be feeling unhappy to write sorrowful music, nor cheerful when creating something with the bounding energy of a Haydn finale. Parts of *Symphonie fantastique* may come over as a feverish outpouring, but that is because they are carefully calculated to create that impression. An artist's life and work are inextricable on one level, but in the act of creating they need not be considered identical.

Politics

Following the July 1830 revolution it was perhaps less surprising that a first prize in the Prix de Rome was offered to a composer clearly in tune with the times (although the vote was not unanimous).[14] In this respect at least, *Symphonie fantastique* was a child of its time, politically and artistically. Understandably, Berlioz felt himself to be on the verge of a breakthrough in Paris, and was reluctant to go to Italy as the conditions of the prize required. His request to be allowed to stay was refused, but he was permitted to shorten his period abroad. The new king, Louis-Philippe, formerly Duc d'Orléans, was head of a family that had long aspired to the throne, but his exiled predecessor's fate, and that of the guillotined Louis XVI, ensured that his reign was less authoritarian. Berlioz was comfortable with the Orléans regime, and benefited from its patronage; members of the royal family supported him, and he received two major government commissions, his mighty Requiem (*Grande Messe des morts*, 1837) and *Symphonie funèbre et triomphale* (1840, the tenth anniversary of the July Revolution).

Fantastic, or Just Atypical?

Maybe both. Having recently encountered Beethoven, Berlioz could not adhere to a late-classical style in succession to Haydn and Mozart. It was odd enough for a young French composer in the 1820s to contemplate writing a symphony. The predominant musical culture was vocal: songs for the salon and dramatic works for the many Paris theatres. These presented different kinds of entertainment: in specialized theatres (government-subsidized and - regulated), this consisted of *grand opéra*, sung throughout, *opéra comique* with spoken dialogue, and Italian opera. Other theatrical entertainments packaged spectacle, music, and dancing in ways that, more than the official theatres, anticipated the preoccupations of romanticism and were more open to foreign influence, for example the adaptation of Weber's opera *Der Freischütz* at the Odéon in 1824.

Berlioz compared his programme to the dialogue in *opéra comique*. A text for the audience to read was a novelty, and it is sometimes asserted that Berlioz drew back, allowing performances in which only the movement titles need be offered to listeners. A note to that effect appeared only in later editions of the symphony, a good twenty years after it was composed; and it was less an aesthetic decision than permission for concert organizers to dispense with the full programme *if necessary* ('à la rigueur').[15] As an impresario himself, Berlioz was permitting his peers, if finances were tight, to economize by printing only movement titles. His preference was for the whole programme to be available, and this was obligatory if the sequel, *Lélio*, was to follow.

This conception was certainly modern in the sense of its being romantic and anti-traditional, like Hugo's dramas and Delacroix's art. Modernity was equally, perhaps more, inherent in the music itself; any debt to recent models (Weber, Beethoven) came about because Berlioz regarded them as modern. Composers after Beethoven, such as Schubert or Felix Mendelssohn, are sometimes perceived as bridging the largely factitious division between classic and romantic styles; their instrumental music may be mostly in classical forms and genres – sonatas, quartets, symphonies – but is often expressive or picturesque (especially Mendelssohn's in overtures and symphonies) in a 'romantic' sense, suggesting evolution of manner rather than a fundamental reappraisal of musical syntax. Romantic composers also wrote many songs; Schubert shared with Berlioz a proclivity for adapting them to instrumental contexts, as in his string quartet in D minor ('Death and the Maiden'). In this he was followed by Robert Schumann, and Mendelssohn went some way to merging genres in his *Songs Without Words*.

An Encounter with Mendelssohn

When he met Felix Mendelssohn in Rome, in 1831, Berlioz, the elder by six years, was still effectively a student, his progress monitored by the Academy. Mendelssohn was a musical thoroughbred, who came to Italy not to study but to tour and gain experience as a musician and visual artist, as he already had in Scotland; he played Berlioz his overture *The Hebrides* (*Fingal's Cave*). Mendelssohn's 'Italian' symphony (No. 4) was performed in 1833, the year before Berlioz's *Harold en Italie*. Berlioz recounted his meeting Mendelssohn in 'letters' written as he toured Germany (1843) for publication in Parisian journals; they are reproduced in his *Mémoires*. He admired Mendelssohn's music and liked him personally; the friendship was mutual, but not the admiration.

It is not known whether Mendelssohn mentioned to Berlioz his recently completed *Reformation Symphony* – known as No. 5, although second in order of composition. It was completed in May 1830, the month of the *Fantastique* rehearsal, though not performed until 1832. Both composers were prone to delay publication until completely satisfied with their work, but Mendelssohn never returned to his *Reformation Symphony*, and it was published posthumously. Both 1830 symphonies quote older religious music, albeit in a very different spirit: Mendelssohn remained a devout Protestant, whereas Berlioz, raised a Roman Catholic despite his father's scepticism, had already lost his faith. Their Italian symphonies are closer in spirit than the *Reformation* is to the *Fantastique*. Both evoke religious processions; in *Harold en Italie* the second movement is headed 'March of Pilgrims singing an evening prayer', while Mendelssohn's second movement has no heading but 'begins with a haunting modal melody evidently meant to depict a religious ceremony or procession'.[16] An incidental connection between these movements, a melodic falling sixth, may be coincidental, but it is possible that these sharp-eared young men had heard something of the kind on their Italian travels. Both are scenic rather than narrative works, but Berlioz, typically, was more specific, referring to mountain scenes and the emotions they evoke, a mountaineer's serenade, and an orgy of brigands.

The *Reformation* has the usual four movements, although the second (Scherzo) and the short slow movement, which is joined to the finale, seem to have little connection to the implicit programme. In the first movement Mendelssohn used two ideas that could have been borrowed from the last symphonies of Mozart (No. 41, 'Jupiter') and Haydn (No. 104, 'London'), but formulae used by these (incidentally Catholic) composers could easily have arisen coincidentally. They may not be programmatically significant; the four-note figure of the slow introduction, often used by Mozart, had also been used twice already by Mendelssohn in his Op. 18 string quintet (1826) and a fugue for string quartet (1827, posthumously published in Op. 81). Haydn's grand slow introduction uses the same notes and a similar rhythm to Mendelssohn's assertive Allegro theme, but they sound very different in context.

Mendelssohn's programme is the struggle for Protestant survival, looking back 300 years to the 'Augsburg Confession' and recalling the struggles of the Thirty Years War (1618–48). The 'Dresden Amen', composed in the late eighteenth century by Johann Gottlieb Naumann for the Catholic court in Dresden, was appropriated by Lutheran churches in Saxony and later used by Liszt in *Vallée d'Obermann* and Wagner in *Parsifal*. Its

Example 2.1 Berlioz, *Grande Messe des morts*,
Dies irae, and the *Dies irae* plainchant

Requiem:
Basses, bars 25-8 (bars 29-32 omitted)

Di - es   i - rae   di - es   il - la

Basses bars 33-6

sae - clum   in   fa-vil - la

Plainchant

Di - es   i - rae,   di - es   il - la

gentle threefold benediction comes before the turbulent Allegro
and again just before the recapitulation. The finale is largely based
on the Lutheran chorale 'Ein feste Burg', a symbol of militant
Protestantism, for which purpose it was also used in Meyerbeer's
Grand opéra Les Huguenots (1836). The chorale opens
Mendelssohn's finale tentatively, on a solo flute, and is heard in
triumph at the end.

Berlioz's first quotation of the *Dies irae* seems respectful,
solemnly intoned on low-pitched instruments and punctuated by
bell-chimes. But he rudely shatters the mood by repeating each
phrase at double speed on trombones, then as a jig on high
woodwind. Having exploited the traditional chant in his finale,
Berlioz was compelled in his Requiem to invent his own plain-
chant-like theme for the text of the chant. To this he adds counterpoints to form the mighty crescendo that leads to the call to
judgement ('Tuba mirum') and the first entry of additional brass
groups, spatially displaced at the corners of the orchestra. The
connection of the *Dies Irae* to his symphony's programme is
obvious: the protagonist has been guillotined, and the black mass
of the finale celebrates his funeral. In the Requiem, Berlioz's
substitute chant uses the same modal scale, with lowered seventh
degree; two bars are identical in pitch. The two are superimposed
in Ex. 2.1.

Fugue

Fugue is also common to the 1830 symphonies. Mendelssohn was fully trained in counterpoint by Carl Friedrich Zelter; Berlioz had studied with Reicha, several of whose published fugues (Op. 36) are remarkably free in construction. Reicha believed that, since other musical elements had evolved in the previous half-century, fugues need not follow the same old rules, but for examination purposes and in line with Conservatoire policy he taught the strict rules and, as Berlioz appreciatively noted, also explained the reasons for them. Berlioz sometimes affected to despise fugue, but what he mostly railed against were routine fugues, inappropriate for their context, notably the rounding-off of the Gloria and Credo in Mass settings with a long fugal 'Amen'. In his Requiem the 'Amen' is soft and mysterious, and he satirized routine 'Amen' fugues in *La Damnation de Faust*, where one is supposedly improvised by students under the influence of Rhenish wine.

Berlioz had nothing against fugues that were expressive and, in vocal music, appropriate for the words. Fugal writing occurs in virtually all his large-scale works, three of which open with fugal passages: *Harold en Italie*, *Roméo et Juliette*, and *La Damnation de Faust*. Fugue figures prominently in the finale of Mendelssohn's *Reformation Symphony*; a fast and taut fugal section suggests continuing struggle before the glowing restatement of 'Ein feste Burg'. In *Symphonie fantastique* Berlioz used fugue satirically in the 'Ronde du Sabbat', his target not Reicha but academicism in general, and perhaps the Conservatoire director Luigi Cherubini, an authoritarian figure with whom Berlioz had clashed. The satire is effective precisely because Berlioz's fugal writing, elsewhere often free, in this instance follows the rules, at least at first. Berlioz was not alone in his suspicion of academic counterpoint; when the conductor François-Antoine Habeneck tried out the *Reformation Symphony* in Paris in 1832, the orchestra of the Société des Concerts 'rejected it as too learned'.[17] But Berlioz found some use for expressive counterpoint in each movement of *Symphonie fantastique* – if not fugue, then fugato, canon, or another favourite device, the combination of themes or motifs first heard separately.

Performance Practice

Berlioz's inventiveness in rhythm and melody are distinctive features of his music that some critics seem to miss, but nearly all acknowledge his genius with the orchestra. He employed a rich palette of colours, mixing and highlighting particular sounds for their expressive qualities. Of course he was not the first to do this in orchestral and dramatic music: in the previous century, his great French predecessor Rameau, but also J. S. Bach, Gluck, and Mozart; nearer to Berlioz's time, early romantic composers, among whom Berlioz would have included Beethoven, as well as Étienne-Nicolas Méhul, and his teachers Jean-François Le Sueur and Antoine Reicha. Perhaps most important in this respect was Carl Maria von Weber, whose best-known opera, *Der Freischütz*, had been staged, albeit considerably altered, at the Odéon in 1824. Its music evoking the demonic surely affected Berlioz's handling of this topic in *Symphonie fantastique* and *La Damnation de Faust*.

Berlioz's concern with timbre highlights a major performance question of our time: to use or not to use the instruments, orchestral layout, and performing practices of *his* time. Much about instruments and layout can be learned from his treatise, but other areas are more difficult to address with confidence, such as string *portamento* unless indicated in the score (*glissando*) and vibrato. We cannot, therefore, resurrect precisely what he had in his mind's ear when composing; but a certain distance can be travelled in that direction with reasonable confidence, helped by Berlioz's meticulous notation.

He defined tempo by the metronome as well as general indications such as allegro, not only at the start of a piece but to control speed-change within a movement. Not every conductor observes these markings scrupulously; the last movement of *Symphonie fantastique* is sometimes mistaken for a chance to show how fast modern orchestras can play, to the detriment of detail or even coherence, for the apparent chaos that so shocked some critical ears early in the work's history makes its fullest effect only when performed with attention to Berlioz's indications of tempo and dynamics.

Berlioz specified the orchestral numbers he wanted, something to be borne in mind even if such forces are not always available. While touring smaller German cities, where he was often well received, he sometimes had to 'make do', substituting piano for harps or clarinet for cor anglais. He also had to accommodate himself to local conditions by playing single movements from his symphonies, choosing those written for smaller forces or that were simply less difficult to get up to scratch in a few rehearsals, rather than insisting on 'all or nothing'.[18]

The orchestra required for *Symphonie fantastique* was not altogether exceptional; the Paris Opéra had considerable forces at its disposal for *grand opéras* by Rossini and Meyerbeer. What was unusual was deploying additional instruments – percussion, woodwind, brass – in a symphony. Beethoven was ahead of Berlioz in requiring these in his Ninth ('Choral') symphony, with three flute players (one on piccolo); Berlioz has two flutes, one also playing piccolo. Beethoven wanted to strengthen the woodwind by doubling each part. Berlioz does not suggest this, but in common with French practice he requires four bassoons. One of the two oboists plays cor anglais, and the other has to begin the third movement playing offstage.

Berlioz's brass section is larger than Beethoven's. To the standard two trumpets and four horns, and the three trombones of the Fifth and Ninth, he adds two cornets and two bass instruments, for which, prior to the development of the tuba family, the options were ophicleide and serpent. Berlioz needed more than the standard two kettledrums, with occasional chords for four of them, requiring two or more players. Besides unpitched percussion (cymbals, bass drum, military (side) drum), Berlioz wanted four harps, two to a part, and he specified *at least* fifteen each of first and second violins and ten violas. More surprising may seem the proportion of nine double basses to eleven cellos.

Large as these forces are, Berlioz resisted the temptation to overuse them. Harps are only used in 'Un Bal', and cor anglais in 'Scène aux champs'. Only one timpanist is needed in the first movement, and none in 'Un Bal'. Trumpets and cornets are not heard until the climax of the first movement, then omitted (with one exception: see below in this section) until the March. The low

25

brass and unpitched percussion are reserved for the March and finale, with bells (or the piano substitute) used only for a section of the latter. The second ophicleide has little to do in the March, to which it was added after the first performance.

In the finale Berlioz originally specified one ophicleide, a keyed brass instrument, and a serpent, made of wood with a brass mouthpiece. Often used in churches, the serpent is suited for the finale's burlesque *Dies Irae*; Berlioz described its sound as better for 'gory Druidic rituals' rather than Christian worship; its widespread use exemplified 'the stupidity, the coarse feeling and taste, that have governed the use of music in our churches since time immemorial'.[19] Mendelssohn also used a serpent in his *Reformation Symphony* finale; like Berlioz, he would probably have replaced it, had he revived the work, with the then modern ophicleide, as more likely to play in tune. The ophicleide in turn was soon rendered obsolete by the tuba. Germany was ahead of France in this development, which Berlioz generally welcomed; his description of the ophicleide in his treatise includes an unflattering likeness of its middle register to 'the cathedral serpent or herdsmen's horns' (as used for a *ranz des vaches*; see Chapter 6). In *Symphonie fantastique* the ophicleide parts do not exploit its lowest notes, which Berlioz considered rough. Rather than a bass tuba, the best modern substitute is a smaller tuba with a relatively narrow bore.

The curious notation of violins at the first movement's climax makes sense if the two sections are seated as was then normal, and as Berlioz assumed and wanted, on either side of the conductor (Ex. 2.2). Each section is *divisi*; the upper and lower lines of each are identical. Berlioz cited this in his treatise (marking it Allegro *assai con fuoco* and *f* rather than *ff*), explaining that he had divided each section to make a difficult passage playable with confidence and strength. The result is a continuous line that is not batted across from left to right and back, as it would be if first violins played the upper part and second violins the lower. The practice, developed during the twentieth century, of seating all the violins on the left, seconds behind the firsts, makes this notation pointless; arguably the whole passage could be played in unison by all the violins. Berlioz, however, who knew the players he was likely to recruit for performances, evidently did not consider this possibility.

Example 2.2 *Symphonie fantastique*, first movement.
Violins I and II from bar 410

Berlioz routinely took advice from professional players. This must especially have affected his writing for 'natural' brass instruments that have to change crook (a detachable length of tubing) to play in different keys. While trumpets were confined to the notes of the natural harmonic series (far apart in the lower range, the gap narrowing as the series ascends), horns could fill some of the gaps between natural or 'open' notes by inserting a hand into the bell. Hand-stopping affects timbre, and so stopped notes could be used deliberately, for effect, rather than (as in Mozart's horn concertos) to increase the number of pitches available. At the start of 'Marche au supplice' Berlioz wanted the hand-stopped (*bouché*) effect. When the score was published, 'cylinders' (or pistons or valves) were becoming available, so that horns could play all the notes evenly as if 'open'; accordingly, he wrote in the published score 'Faites les sons bouchés avec la main, sans employer les cylindres' ('play stopped notes with the hand without using cylinders'). In his treatise, he described the quality of hand-stopped notes on a scale from very bad to good; some notes, muffled if played quietly, are explosive in *forte*. He illustrated the dramatic effects of stopped notes in a passage by Méhul for four natural horns in different keys.[20] Elsewhere Berlioz himself used four horns in different keys to increase the open notes available, but for most of *Symphonie fantastique* he adopted the usual arrangement: two

27

pairs of horns in different keys suited to each movement (in the first and last, C and E♭). Horns in three keys are prescribed for 'Scène aux champs' to obtain a few more open notes, but the third, in E♭, changes to F before the end. Berlioz deplored lazy players of the new chromatic horns who played every note as if it were 'open', regardless of the sound composers wanted. His sinister 'Marche au supplice' is enhanced by unequal tone-quality at the start; the *sons bouchés* include accented notes (e.g. the first horn's first note). He would also have condemned another lazy practice resorted to by some modern players, of simply muting the instrument; a consistent muted sound is not identical to the varied timbre of stopped notes.

So much for instruments; this is a work that requires a conductor, preferably one who takes careful note of Berlioz's performance directions, not least metronome markings. We live in a period where listeners to recorded music, at least works recorded as often as *Symphonie fantastique*, can select the conductors whose work they like, some working with 'period-instrument' ensembles, some with entirely modern instruments and – in an interesting 'third way' – others persuading modern orchestras to employ at least some of what are known as HIP (historically informed performance) practices.

In his book *Conducting Berlioz* and its companion volumes, Norman del Mar, a conductor with a wide repertory, offers much sage advice and many trenchant observations on tempi and on instruments (modern) and how they are to be used, and identifies potential pitfalls. Regrettably, some 'maestros' have provided justification for the epithet 'flashy' that I have seen applied to *Symphonie fantastique*, but which seems singularly inapt even for its less introspective passages. This, however, is not del Mar's intention in calling the work 'a virtuoso piece for conductor and orchestra alike'. Virtuosity is not the same as showing off, and is best directed towards delivering the music's essence. Indeed, he suggests that the third movement's *ranz des vaches* should mostly be played 'without the distraction of the conductor's monitoring', allowing the player freedom to make it sound spontaneous, although the conductor may have to monitor the few other instruments involved.

In the finale, del Mar notes Berlioz's instruction that two timpanists should play the single bass drum ('another historical element in the development of the orchestra'), and comments on the pitch and location of the bells: tubular bells are 'never deep or sonorous enough' for the ominous ritual within the finale. Berlioz wanted them offstage ('derrière la scène'), and notated their entries on two staves as if for piano, with this note: 'If bells are not available, use several pianos on the stage' ('sur l'avant-scène'). The highest pitch notated is middle C (c'), doubled by the two octaves below it (c, C), precluding the higher chimes that are usually heard.

Del Mar includes many notes on the shortcomings of the Breitkopf 'complete' edition of Berlioz's works, now well over a century old.[21] Although its volumes have been reprinted as miniature scores by Kalmus, they have been superseded by the New Berlioz Edition (NBE) published by Bärenreiter, which is closer to the composer's apparent intentions and is actually complete. Del Mar was not the first to point out that the Breitkopf editors, the librarian and musicologist Charles Malherbe and the conductor and composer Felix Weingartner, pursued a policy that modern scholars reject: homogenization by updating according to their contemporary (post-Wagnerian) notational practices and eliminating apparent discrepancies in phrasing or dynamics even when these were carefully notated in Berlioz's manuscript and printed scores. Like poetry, music can suffer by such apparently logical proceedings, especially when dealing with a composer like Berlioz who left little to chance; he wanted his music, as Igor Stravinsky might have put it, not to be interpreted, but to be *played*.[22]

***

Berlioz's symphony was first published in 1834 in the form of a piano transcription ('partition de piano') by his younger friend and colleague Franz Liszt. Liszt also produced a short piece entitled *L'idée fixe, Andante amoroso* (1833), which sets the principal theme of the symphony with an idiomatically pianistic accompaniment. It would make a charming recital encore; however, it is not a transcription but one of Liszt's many original works that elaborate another composer's material, using harmonies untypical of Berlioz.

Liszt's transcription of the entire *Symphonie fantastique* is a creative act of a different kind, with no new harmonies. He also transcribed *Harold en Italie* and an opera, *Esmeralda* by Louise Bertin, with a libretto by Hugo from his *Notre-Dame de Paris*. An operatic vocal score has a practical use for rehearsal, as does the *Harold* transcription for the solo viola player, who can usefully learn the work with a pianist representing the orchestra. But if the *Symphonie fantastique* transcription had a purpose, it was less for preparing performances than for study, and to make the work known. There are many indications of instrumentation that do little to assist a pianist tackling its many technical difficulties but suggest that Liszt had grasped the importance of timbre for Berlioz's expressive intentions. The first extensive published study of Berlioz's work, by Robert Schumann (see Chapter 10), was undertaken using this transcription; Schumann had neither seen the orchestral score nor heard the symphony.

Nevertheless, because the texture of *Symphonie fantastique* is so orchestrally idiomatic, the transcription is not always literal. One can hardly blame Liszt for some decisions intended to replicate the effect of an orchestra in pianistic terms. He sends some passages up an octave for brilliance, and represents some darker sonorities by downward octave transposition. Oscillating chords (the 'Liszt trill') replace fast tremolo on repeated notes. He does his best with the *col legno* passage in the finale (from bar 443; see Chapter 8) by using both hands above the treble staff, but has to compromise after a few bars when the cellos enter beneath by simplifying the right-hand rhythms.

Liszt actually performed parts of his transcription in Berlioz's own concerts (1834, 1836). He revised it after Berlioz's death for a second edition (1876).[23] 'Marche au supplice' was published separately in 1866, and the original version altered, possibly to suit more modern pianos. In bars 79 and 81 Liszt attacks a dissonant bass note (E♭) eight times per bar against the first edition's (and Berlioz's) two, and replaces a full right-hand chord with a flurry of arpeggios. The last change is one Berlioz would hardly have sanctioned; he had objected to Liszt changing note values in the overture *Le Roi Lear* to make his transcription playable up to speed. Despite the difficulty of the *Symphonie fantastique* transcription, and despite numerous orchestral recordings, some courageous pianists continue to tackle, even to record, Liszt's monochrome version.

Most of those attracted to Berlioz's symphony no doubt prefer the polychromatic original. There are too many orchestral recordings of *Symphonie fantastique* properly to review here, but a few may be considered of especial interest. Unfortunately, performances conducted by his fellow composers Gustav Mahler and Sergei Rachmaninoff took place before the era of recording. There followed many celebrated conductors with an evident affection for the work, including Arturo Toscanini, Hamilton Harty, Thomas Beecham, John Barbirolli, Charles Munch, and Pierre Monteux, but there are also excellent recordings by conductors from more recent generations.

Jean Martinon made a fine recording with a French orchestra before its adoption of 'German' bassoons, so with bassoon tone nearer to what Berlioz would have heard; this recording has the advantage of being coupled with the sequel, *Lélio*. This coupling was also recorded by Pierre Boulez, whose performances are widely admired for their clarity. Colin Davis recorded nearly all of Berlioz's music, much of it twice; his versions of the symphony and *Lélio* are strongly recommended. Among those active at the time of writing, John Nelson and François-Xavier Roth are rightly admired for idiomatic and dynamic performances of Berlioz; Roth has directed performances enthusiastically received at the annual Berlioz Festival in the composer's birthplace, La Côte-Saint-André.

Among recordings using period-instrument orchestras (including real ophicleides) is John Eliot Gardiner's (1993, Philips) with the Orchestre Révolutionnaire et Romantique. This was preceded by Roger Norrington's (1989, EMI) with the London Classical Players. Norrington prepared for this by arranging and directing an immersive Berlioz Weekend in London that included *Symphonie fantastique* and *Roméo et Juliette*.

More than just period instruments, which even so devoted a Berliozian as Davis preferred not to use, are needed for a 'historically informed' performance. Norrington is one who took careful account of composers' intentions even when performing with modern orchestras; some have taken exception to his tempi, ironically, because he adhered scrupulously to Berlioz's metronome markings. The reception of performance is, rightly, a matter of taste. Berlioz's attention to detail anticipates many early twentieth-century composers, but as is often noticed, even users of the metronome as diverse in style as Elgar and Stravinsky did not always stick to their own metronome markings in their recordings. We cannot know to what extent that may have been true of Berlioz, since all that survives from him is the set of performance instructions known as the score, but we can do our best to represent his musical intentions in line with what we understand, from the programme, to have been his 'meaning'.

Notes

1. Théophile Gautier (1811–72) in *La Presse* (7 December 1846, the day after the premiere of Berlioz's *La Damnation de Faust*).
2. Lorenz Eitner, 'Introduction to Delacroix', in *Delacroix: An Exhibition of Paintings, Drawings and Lithographs Arranged by the Arts Council of Great Britain in Association with the Edinburgh Festival Society*, Edinburgh Festival exhibition catalogue (N.p.: The Arts Council, 1964), 7.
3. Hector Berlioz, 'Aperçu sur la musique classique et romantique', in *Le Correspondant* (22 October 1830). In Berlioz, *Hector Berlioz, Critique musicale 1823–1863*, Vol. I, 63–8, ed. H. Robert Cohen and Yves Gerard (Paris: Société française de musicologie, 1996, 2001). Translation in *Berlioz on Music: Selected Criticism 1824–1837*, ed. Katherine Kolb, trans. Samuel N. Rosenberg (New York: Oxford University Press, 2015), 34–40.
4. Jean-François Marmontel, *Essai sur les revolutions de la musique en France* (1777), reprinted in François Lesure (ed.), *Querelle des Gluckistes et des Piccinnistes* (Geneva: Minkoff, 1984), Vol. 1, 180–1.
5. Hoffmann, *Review of Beethoven's Fifth Symphony*.
6. Bernstein, in *The Unanswered Question* (Charles Eliot Norton lectures, 1973), lecture 4 ('The Delights and Dangers of Ambiguity'), c. thirty-five minutes into the lecture (available on YouTube: www.youtube.com/watch?v=hwXO3I8ASSg.
7. *CG* Vol. V, 601, *CG* Vol. VI, 436.
8. Charles Rosen and Henri Zerner, *Romanticism and Realism*, 74.

9. Mark Evan Bonds, *The Beethoven Syndrome: Hearing Music as Autobiography* (New York: Oxford University Press, 2020).
10. Scott Burnham, *Beethoven Hero* (Princeton, NJ: Princeton University Press, 1995), 113.
11. Hector Berlioz, *À travers chants: Études musicales, adorations, boutades et critiques* (Paris: Michel Lévy frères, 1862), 33; ed. Léon Guichard (Paris: Gründ, 1971), 51.
12. *Mémoires* (ed. Bloom), 226–7; *The Memoirs* (trans. Cairns), 71–2.
13. 'Il faut tâcher de faire froidement les choses brûlantes.' Letter to Princess Wittgenstein, 12 August 1856. *CG* Vol. V, 352–3; translation of this letter, David Cairns, *Berlioz*, Vol. II, *Servitude and Greatness* (London: Allen Lane, the Penguin Press, 1999), 608–9.
14. Peter Bloom, 'Berlioz and the Prix de Rome of 1830', *Journal of the American Musicological Society* 34 (1981): 279–304.
15. NBE 16, 170. See Nicholas Temperley, 'The "Symphonie fantastique" and Its Program', *Musical Quarterly* 57 (1971): 593–608.
16. R. Larry Todd, 'Mendelssohn', in Stanley Sadie and John Tyrrell (eds.), *The New Grove Dictionary of Music and Musicians* (London: Macmillan, 2001), Vol. 16, 403.
17. R. Larry Todd, *Mendelssohn: A Life in Music* (New York: Oxford University Press, 2003), 254.
18. See Berlioz, *Mémoires*, which reproduces letters for the Parisian press from his tours of Germany and Austria.
19. See Hector Berlioz, *Grand Traité d'instrumentation et d'orchestration modernes* (Paris: Schonenberger, 1843); ed. and annotated by Peter Bloom, NBE 24 (Kassel: Bärenreiter, 2003), 355. English edition: Berlioz, *Berlioz's Orchestration Treatise: A Translation and Commentary, ed. and trans Hugh Macdonald* (Cambridge: Cambridge University Press, 2002), 172.
20. Berlioz, *Grand Traité* (ed. Peter Bloom), 269. Macdonald, *Berlioz's Orchestration Treatise*, 170–2.
21. Norman del Mar, *Conducting Berlioz* (Oxford: Clarendon Press, 1997), 1–51; cited 3, 23, 39, 42.
22. Hector Berlioz, *Werke*, ed. Charles Malherbe and Felix Weingartner (Leipzig: Breitkopf und Härtel, 1900–7). Errors in the edition are listed in Jacques Barzun, *Berlioz and the Romantic Century*, 2nd edition (New York: Columbia University Press, 1969), Vol. 2, 359–81.
23. Second edition revised by Liszt, Leipzig 1876. Prior to that, editions published outside France included Vienna 1836, Leipzig 1844–5, and Milan 1846.

3

SYMPHONIE FANTASTIQUE IN BERLIOZ'S LIFETIME

The sources of the experience that shaped *Symphonie fantastique* are diverse and complex, but may be grouped under three headings: biographical, musical, and literary. Biographical sources comprise Berlioz's health, his love life, and the musical and literary discoveries he compared to thunderbolts (*coups de foudre*).[1] Musical sources include his practice of recycling his own work, as well as influences from earlier music. Literary influences include older authors such as Florian, contemporaries such as Hugo, Goethe's *Faust*, and above all Shakespeare.

Recycling in *Symphonie fantastique*

Berlioz himself drew attention to his use of a Florian poem for the opening Largo (see Chapter 1). The foreshadowing of the *idée fixe* in *Herminie* became known when the cantata was published in the centenary of Berlioz's birth.[2] The autograph of the *Messe solennelle* resurfaced as recently as 1992, revealing several ideas used in later works, among them the main theme of the third movement ('Scène aux champs').[3] The other known self-borrowing is the whole fourth movement ('Marche au supplice'), composed for *Les Francs-juges*, an opera that preoccupied Berlioz for nearly a decade. He was reworking it in 1829, hoping the Paris Opéra might take an interest, although France's premier opera house was unlikely to accept a work by a student composer and an unknown librettist (Ferrand). In his letter outlining the symphony's programme, Berlioz refrained from telling his friend that the march had previously been intended for their joint project.

A Literary Thunderbolt: Shakespeare

In 1827 and 1828 Berlioz experienced cultural shocks that permanently altered his intellectual and emotional landscape. What he called 'the supreme drama of my life' is a tale often told. In September 1827 he was bowled over by performances of *Hamlet* and *Romeo and Juliet* by an English troupe at the Odéon theatre, and he fell in love with Harriet Smithson, who played Ophelia and Juliet. His words quoted here were not all that he could say, of course, and they contain a characteristic bit of self-deflation:

The impression she made on my heart and mind by her extraordinary talent, nay her dramatic genius, was equalled by the havoc wrought in me by the poet she so nobly interpreted. That is all I can say.

Shakespeare, coming upon me unawares, struck me like a thunderbolt. . . . I lost the power of sleep, and with it all my former animation, all taste for my favourite studies, all ability to work. . . . As I came out of *Hamlet*, shaken to the depths by the experience, I vowed not to expose myself a second time to the flame of Shakespeare's genius. Next day the playbills announced *Romeo and Juliet*. . . . I rushed round to the box-office the moment I saw the posters and bought a stall.[4]

He denied a report that he had left the theatre after *Romeo and Juliet* exclaiming 'I shall marry that woman and write my greatest symphony on the play', adding 'I did both, but I never said anything of the sort'.[5] Yet it is possible that he considered an orchestral response to *Romeo and Juliet* even before composing *Symphonie fantastique*.[6]

In 1827 Berlioz knew little if any English, but the theatre made bilingual texts available, with 'traditional' alterations derived from eighteenth-century practice, such as David Garrick's Drury Lane productions; Berlioz based some of his *Roméo et Juliette* on that version. He did not risk seeing the 1827 *Othello*, with Harriet Smithson as Desdemona; one can only imagine his feelings had he seen her strangled in a manner 'blatantly savage, and Kemble compounded the horror by taking his time about it . . . adding two gratuitous *coups de grâce* with his dagger'.[7] But he was soon reading the plays in French, and *Othello* may have played a role in the formation of the symphony; jealousy, mentioned in connection with the first movement, causes the protagonist's mental storm in the third.[8] In 1829 he quoted *Hamlet* and *Romeo and*

35

Juliet in English on his own scores (*Huit Scènes de Faust* and *Cléopâtre*).[9] Working over *Symphonie fantastique* in Italy, having just read *King Lear*, he wrote on the title page the French translation of 'As flies to wanton boys are we to the gods'.[10]

This was early in 1831, following a different kind of thunderbolt. On the rebound from Smithson's refusal even to meet him, he had become engaged to Camille Moke. Jilted by letter (she married a wealthier man), he planned a terrible vengeance, but en route to Paris he recovered his sense of proportion, and of humour. He recuperated in Nice where he composed his *Grande Ouverture du Roi Lear*, with expansive themes for Cordelia, a role that had also been taken by Smithson. His unrequited love for 'Henriette' (as he called her) has become the stuff of legend, but the conception of the 'return to life' (*Lélio*) also reflects his recovery from the blow of his broken engagement.

Musical Thunderbolts

When Berlioz saw Weber's *Der Freischütz* at the Odéon theatre in 1824, under the title *Robin des bois*, he studied the original score and deplored the alterations that perhaps helped it to succeed in France. When asked to compose recitatives for a new production at the Opéra (1841), he scrupulously refused an invitation to use his own music for the obligatory ballet, preferring to orchestrate a piano piece by Weber. He greatly admired Weber's romantic opera about ordinary people affected by diabolical intervention, as is most clearly manifest in *La Damnation de Faust*, but Weber's dramatic orchestration already affected *Les Francs-juges* as well as *Symphonie fantastique*. But it was not Weber's symphonies, which he is unlikely to have known, that provided the stimulus to cast his personal feelings in symphonic form.

In 1828 the professional Société des Concerts du Conservatoire was formed, beginning a series of performances that endured well into the twentieth century.[11] It was directed by a dominant figure in Parisian music, the violinist and conductor François-Antoine Habeneck, who also conducted at the Opéra. Habeneck insisted on thorough rehearsals, and he centred the Société's early repertoire on symphonies and overtures by Beethoven. The Société itself performed very little by Berlioz in his lifetime; Habeneck conducted Berlioz premieres, including *Symphonie fantastique*, in the concert hall of the Conservatoire, and the orchestra may have included some of the same musicians, but these concerts were organized and promoted by Berlioz himself at his own financial peril.

Berlioz developed into one of the major conductors of his time, performing his own and others' music in France, Germany, the Austrian Empire, Russia, and London. But in the 1830s Habeneck, as the official conductor of state-sponsored events, would have been more likely to impress a potential audience. His reputation has been tarnished by the report that in 1837 he took a pinch of snuff at a critical juncture in Berlioz's *Grande Messe des morts* (*Requiem*). The story has been disputed, although it was witnessed; it was perhaps at the general rehearsal rather than the premiere.[12] But Berlioz gave Habeneck due credit for helping him with *Symphonie fantastique* and entrusted him with what could have been a sensational posthumous second performance. Contemplating suicide once he had murdered his faithless fiancée, he wrote a letter to Habeneck to accompany the revised score. Habeneck directed the 1832 performance, and the premiere of *Lélio*.

Berlioz attended the Société's early concerts, hearing excellent performances of Beethoven's *Eroica*, Fifth, and *Pastoral* symphonies which, with the Ninth (*Choral*), were those he valued most highly. His admiration is reflected in a general study of Beethoven (1829) and essays on the symphonies (1838), republished in his third collection of essays, *À travers chants* (1862). He has been called 'one of the most important critics in the early reception of Beethoven'.[13] But he did not take Beethoven as a direct model for his own work. The *Pastoral*, like the *Fantastique*, although it is in five movements rather than the usual four, has no slow introduction; nor do the other Beethoven symphonies mentioned above. Berlioz's 'Scène aux champs' has echoes, but no more, of Beethoven's 'Scene by the brook' (see Chapter 6). Aspects of *Harold en Italie* and *Roméo et Juliette* take a lead, but again little more than that, from Beethoven's Ninth.

Beethoven's Fifth upset Berlioz's composition teacher Jean-François Le Sueur (1760–1837); overwhelmed by the performance, he told Berlioz the next day that 'such music ought not be written'. Berlioz assured him that there was little danger of anything else like it being composed.[14] He cannot have failed to notice that Beethoven's symphonies tend to be directed towards a culminating finale. The Fifth is an archetype of the trajectory called *per ardua ad astra* – triumph through striving. In *Symphonie fantastique* Berlioz reversed this trajectory; although hardly a tragic symphony, its ending is no triumph.[15]

Berlioz had no obvious precedent for pouring his innermost feelings into this form. French symphonies from the *ancien régime*, like those of the prolific and recently deceased François-Joseph Gossec (1734–1829), would not interest a composer smitten with Beethoven. Cherubini's 1815 symphony was written for London. Jean Mongrédien points out that around the turn of the century French composers exhibited a 'disaffection' with the symphony, 'turning away from a form where they could no doubt have collected many laurels'.[16] Berlioz admired some Méhul operas because, as with Weber, he used orchestral colour dramatically. Méhul's symphonies (composed between 1797 and 1810) are fine works, but there is no great likelihood that Berlioz knew them; however Méhul did anticipate many nineteenth-century symphonies by connecting movements thematically. As for Le Sueur, at least before 1828 he would probably have associated the word *symphonie* with orchestral scene-setting in operas.

More important for Berlioz was a changing perception of listening, strongly affected by Beethoven.[17] It was pioneered in criticism by Hoffmann in his 1810 review of the Fifth Symphony, although he offered no support for programmes; on the contrary, his essay exemplifies an aesthetic position that maintained that the 'truly romantic' lay in 'pure' instrumental music, without literary or picturesque titles. Symphonies were not mere entertainment; they should be attended to in silence, and take us out of ourselves and the everyday world, connecting us to the 'sublime' which is beyond the power of words.

Composers pay no heed to such arguments; many nineteenth-century and early twentieth-century composers produced quantities of instrumental music with and without titles or programmes. Perceptions of a narrative trajectory in Beethoven symphonies, moreover, may seem to contradict Hoffmann and threaten the very possibility of 'pure' ('abstract', non-referential) music. The Fifth's culminating finale reprises the sinister Scherzo; the preceding movements are quoted and banished in the finale of the Ninth. Such cross-references, common in later composers (Anton Bruckner, César Franck), had already affected Mendelssohn before the *Reformation* symphony, in his precocious Octet (1825), and were adopted by Robert Schumann in his Third Symphony (*Rhenish*) and his untitled Second; in this respect, Berlioz was typical of nineteenth-century symphonic thinking.

Theatrical and Literary Influences

Berlioz conformed more to the preferences of his teachers, fellow-composers, and the public when he wrote songs ('romances') and dramatic and choral music. In 1830 his songs and choruses after Thomas Moore were published as Op. 2, and he produced other choral music and cantatas in addition to his Prix de Rome offerings. But his main aspiration was towards opera, and not only because success would bring financial rewards. This was the era of *grand opéra*: tragedies on historical themes, often in five acts, superbly sung and staged, with choruses, ballets, and rich orchestration. The genre is now associated with Meyerbeer, but before 1830 the most successful examples were by Auber (*La Muette de Portici*) and Rossini (*Guillaume Tell*), staged in 1829. By that year, Berlioz had abandoned at least one other opera besides *Les Francs-juges*; perhaps *Estelle et Némorin* (after Florian) would have included the melody he re-used to open *Symphonie fantastique*, a tribute to his 'Stella montis'.

After his first two symphonies, Berlioz completed three operas and two dramatic works for concert performance, *La Damnation de Faust* (1846) and *L'Enfance du Christ* (1850–4), both of which have been staged, like Johann Wolfgang Goethe's two-part verse tragedy *Faust*; the latter was written as a play but was most likely to have been experienced on the written page. In 1828 Berlioz read *Faust* Part I, translated by Gérard de Nerval (1808–55), also a doctor's son and a friend of Gautier; his was the third French translation, and the best. Goethe's drama included lyrics designed for music, and Berlioz used Nerval's translations in setting nine of them, two being run together, in *Huit Scènes de Faust* (published as Op. 1).

Later in 1829, a play based on *Faust* with music, dance, and spectacular scenery was shown at the suburban Théâtre de la Porte-Saint-Martin. Berlioz told his sister 'They've blasphemed *Faust* by turning it into a worthless melodrama.'[18] Soon after, he angled for a commission for a *Faust* ballet, writing to the Minister of Fine Arts, Vicomte Sosthène de la Rochefoucauld.[19] This came to nothing, but there are hints of *Faust* in *Symphonie fantastique* and it is possible that some of the music first came to his mind in that connection. Goethe's 'Walpurgisnacht' is a sort of witches' Sabbath on the Brocken mountains; a demon appears in the form of Faust's lover Gretchen, which must have suggested the arrival of the beloved in Berlioz's finale, with the *idée fixe* distorted and trivialized. An earlier *Faust* translation by Albert Stapfer was republished in 1828 with engravings by Delacroix that Berlioz could have seen, including the vision in the 'Walpurgisnacht' (see Figure 3.1). Berlioz's choice of plainchant in his finale seems natural in this context, but could also have been suggested by the Cathedral scene in *Faust*: Gretchen tries to pray while an evil spirit threatens her with damnation; meanwhile a choir, unseen and so possibly imaginary, sings the *Dies irae*.

The most telling evidence for Goethe's influence on *Symphonie fantastique* comes as early as February 1829. Shortly before the publication of *Huit Scènes*, Berlioz told Ferrand that he was contemplating a 'descriptive symphony on *Faust*'.[20] This need not imply that musical ideas were written down and subsequently used in *Symphonie fantastique*, although that is possible. But this unrealized project means that Berlioz was already thinking of composing a programmatic symphony; some such work on *Faust* later interested Wagner, resulting in his *Faust* overture (1840), and was realized by Liszt (1854).

Other literary sources possibly at the back of Berlioz's mind when planning *Symphonie fantastique* have been identified by

Figure 3.1 Eugène Delacroix, *Gretchen and Faust, Walpurgisnacht* (*c*. 1828), showing the apparition of Gretchen

Nicholas Temperley.[21] These include Chateaubriand's *René*, whose phrase 'vague des passions' is cited in Berlioz's preamble to the programme.[22] The French noun 'vague' is 'wave', but as an adjective it also translates as the English 'vague'. Either would fit Berlioz's programme: a wave-like flux of emotion, and the uncertainty of longing for an unobtainable other (Estelle Dubœuf, Harriet Smithson, or both). Berlioz uses 'vague' in the Preface to *Roméo et Juliette*, where he claims that for the scenes he had in mind (especially the love scene) the 'vague' of instrumental music was 'incomparably more powerful' than vocal music.[23] Temperley cites Victor Hugo's ballad *La Ronde du Sabbat* (compare the title of Berlioz's finale), to which might be added Hugo's 1829 monologue of a man about to be executed (*Le Dernier Jour d'un condamné*), a further indication of the interest romantic artists sometimes showed in matters an older aesthetic might have excluded as morbid and tasteless.

Ten lines from the first poem in Hugo's *Feuilles d'automne* are also written on the autograph title-page of Berlioz's symphony. The poem was published in 1831, but written in 1830, so Berlioz might have seen a copy and added the words when in Rome, or later.

My soul, more than a weary dotard lacking ambition, would surely turn pale on looking into the abyss of my thoughts: all I've suffered, all I've experienced, all that's deceived me like under-ripe fruit; my best years are over, with no hope of reviving the loves, the work, the sorrows of youth; at the age when the future smiles, every page of the book of my life is written.[24]

This rough paraphrase of untranslatable lines suggests how they might have resonated with Berlioz's disillusion following his rejection by Estelle, Harriet, and Camille, although he was past thinking of suicide. Under-ripe fruit suggests unrealized projects, but like his alter ego Lélio, he was determined to work on and achieve his ambition to create 'great works' at any cost; despite the successful premiere of *Roméo et Juliette*, in 1841 he wrote to his sister Nancy 'C'est la grande musique qui me ruine'.[25]

Temperley also reproduces passages added by Alfred de Musset to his translation (1828) of Thomas de Quincey's *Confessions of an English Opium Eater*. Berlioz's medical education had acquainted him with the effects of opium, which both he and his father (the doctor) sometimes used to relieve pain.

Berlioz was an avid reader, but as he left no diary of his literary explorations we cannot know exactly what he read and when. Letters to his sister prior to 1830 recommend novels read in translation (Walter Scott, Fenimore Cooper).[26] The symphony's title was possibly influenced by translations of Hoffmann's tales as *Contes fantastiques*; they were admired and imitated by French writers like Charles Nodier (who contributed to the *Faust* melodrama) and Gautier. Francesca Brittan notes that 'fantasy was perceived as both a literary and a musical mode', owing much to Hoffmann's invocations of music; his combination of fiction and music criticism would have appealed to Berlioz, who wrote his own 'contes fantastiques', short fictions involving music reproduced in his *Evenings in the Orchestra* (*Les Soirées de l'orchestre*, 1852).[27]

Performance and Revision

Symphonie fantastique was eventually performed on 5 December 1830 with other works by Berlioz: the *Francs-juges* overture, two choruses from his *Mélodies irlandaises*, and his Rome Prize cantata *Sardanapale*. This concert was for charity, not for his own profit, with players from theatre orchestras and the Société des concerts who were unpaid. Berlioz's description of the concert in his memoirs is brief, and leads to a tirade against the critics and academicians who misrepresented his intentions and his music, whereas young people understood him even if they were not musicians.[28] But the initial reception was good; the audience demanded an encore of the March (which had to be declined), liked the waltz, and was interested in the finale. Little is said about the first movement, but 'Scène aux champs' was not appreciated; these were the movements most thoroughly revised when Berlioz was in Italy.[29]

Berlioz's profile had been raised by the performance of his *Tempest* fantasy in a concert at the Opéra on 7 November, and the December audience included notable musicians as well as his fiancée Camille Moke. He considered repeating the programme before leaving for Italy, with himself conducting, but wiser counsels prevailed; he would have had to pay the musicians, even supposing they were willing to take part.

Most early reviews were little more than statements that the event had taken place, and the distinguished editor of *La Revue musicale*, François-Joseph Fétis, though puzzled, managed to say a few kind words.[30] It was only in 1835 that Fétis chose to write about the symphony at greater length, and with considerable venom; Schumann saw his article and responded to it in his own periodical (see Chapter 10). By 1835 Fétis bore a grudge; Berlioz had mortally offended him in one of the monologues of *Lélio*. At the 1832 premiere, the audience identified his unnamed target and reacted with 'laughter and applause'.[31] Fétis correctly took this to refer to his own 'improvements' to Beethoven's symphonies, and in 1835 he replied in kind (see Chapter 9).

Berlioz tended to overwrite, and many of his revisions in this and other works are cuts. The *Symphonie fantastique* performed in 1830 has not survived; such changes as can be identified are referred to in Chapters 4–8. For his revisions to 'Scène aux champs' Berlioz thanked Ferdinand Hiller for advice (this was gracious of Hiller, since he had lost his girlfriend, Camille Moke, to Berlioz).

After making revisions and hearing the 1832 performance, Berlioz allowed his friend Liszt to transcribe the whole symphony. It is ironic that this path-breaking work of orchestral thinking and colour was first published as a *partition de piano*. Further detailed changes followed, but despite the best efforts of scholars, the original forms of the first and third movements are irrecoverable.[32] Berlioz continued refining his work until he was ready to release the full score for publication, along with printed orchestral parts. After that, in an age not much concerned with intellectual property rights, anyone who could purchase the material could perform it. Berlioz had delayed publication to introduce his work to a wider audience, so that some who planned their own performances might at least have heard it under the composer's direction. Hence publication came after performances in Belgium and Germany, as well as Paris. The published score bears a dedication to the Tsar Nicholas I, in anticipation of a future visit to Russia; this took place in 1847 with considerable success, not least financial.

In 1833 Berlioz was still not ready to take over from more experienced conductors. Narcisse Girard directed the three middle movements of the symphony in May and the whole work in December. He must have acquitted himself reasonably well, as Berlioz entrusted him with two concerts in November 1834, the first including *Symphonie fantastique*, the second the premiere of *Harold en Italie*. These concerts, organized by Berlioz (who also joined the percussion section) were successful, even bringing in some money. In the following winter season Girard directed Berlioz's first concert, but his occasional failings were beginning to exasperate the composer, who himself conducted *Symphonie fantastique* on 13 December 1835. In 1838, soon after the first performances of *Benvenuto Cellini*, Berlioz organized two concerts, both including *Symphonie fantastique*; on 25 November he was ill and Habeneck conducted, but Berlioz returned to conduct it on 16 December. These concerts, still taking place in the Conservatoire's concert hall, also included works by other composers.[33]

In later years, newer works such as *Roméo et Juliette* and *La Damnation de Faust* tended to displace earlier works in Berlioz's programmes, but when he first ventured abroad the score and orchestral parts of *Symphonie fantastique* were in his baggage. It was performed in Brussels (October 1842), then in various German cities, not always complete and with adjustments to instrumentation (see Chapter 2); a complete performance was given in Dresden (February 1843). Following publication of the score, Berlioz gave performances, again not all complete, in Vienna, Prague, and Budapest (1845–6). He wrote from Prague that he heard tunes from the symphony sung in the streets, one being the waltz. In this letter he notated two others that formed, he says, a 'musical argot' exchanged between young men in the street to characterize the women they encountered. The *idée fixe* in its chaste original form means she is charming ('charmante'). The finale's parody means she is common and bold ('elle a l'air commun et hardi'). The first movement's oboe solo (also quoted) suggests a person – male, as the adjective makes clear – who is sad and anxious ('triste et inquiet').[34]

When he eventually travelled to Russia, Berlioz was most concerned to redeem *La Damnation de Faust* from its initially cool reception in Paris, but he included *Symphonie fantastique* in his last concert (St Petersburg, 20 May 1847). It was then somewhat neglected until performed with its sequel *Lélio* in one of the 'Berlioz weeks' organized by Liszt in Weimar (21 February 1855); this was the last performance of the whole 'Episode in the life of an artist' in Berlioz's lifetime. He conducted the symphony again in St Petersburg (7 December 1867), but this time his farewell concert (8 February 1868 and his last concert anywhere) ended with *Harold en Italie*. After he died, *Symphonie fantastique* took pride of place among his most popular works, with *La Damnation* and the concert overture *Le Carnaval romain*, and so it has remained.

Notes

1. *Mémoires*, chap. 18.
2. Hector Berlioz, *Werke*, Abtheilung I/1, *Symphonie fantastique* (Leipzig: Breitkopf und Härtel, 1900).

3. Hugh Macdonald, 'Berlioz's Messe solennelle', *19th-Century Music* 16 (Spring 1993): 267–85.

4. 'L'effet de son prodigieux talent, ou plûtot de son génie dramatique, sur mon imagination et sur mon cœur, n'est comparable qu'au bouleversement que me fit subir le poète dont elle était la digne interprète. Je ne puis rien dire de plus./Shakespeare, en tombant ainsi sur moi à l'improviste, me foudroya. ... En sortant de la représentation d'*Hamlet*, épouvanté de ce que j'avais ressenti, je m'étais promis formellement de ne pas m'exposer de nouveau à la flamme shakespearienne./Le lendemain on afficha *Romeo and Juliet* ... je courus au bureau de location acheter une stalle'. *Mémoires* (ed. Bloom), 225–6; *The Memoirs* (trans. Cairns), 70, 72.

5. *Illustrated London News*, 12 February 1848; *Mémoires*, chap. 18.

6. Hugh Macdonald, 'Berlioz's Lost *Roméo et Juliette*', in Peter Bloom (ed.), *Berlioz: Scenes from the Life and Work* (Rochester, NY: University of Rochester Press, 2008), 125–37.

7. Peter Raby, '*Fair Ophelia*': *The Life of Harriet Smithson Berlioz* (Cambridge: Cambridge University Press, 1982), 79.

8. Katherine Kolb, 'Berlioz's *Othello*', in David Charlton and Katharine Ellis (eds.), *The Musical Voyager: Berlioz in Europe*, Perspektiven der Opernforschung 14 (Frankfurt am Main: Peter Lang, 2007), 241–62.

9. See Julian Rushton, 'Shakespeare in Berlioz, Berlioz in Shakespeare', in Christopher Wilson and Mervyn Cooke (eds.), *The Oxford Handbook of Shakespeare and Music* (New York: Oxford University Press, 2022), 607–23.

10. *King Lear*, Act IV, scene 1. Facsimile, NBE 16, 182: 'Nous sommes aux dieux ce que sont les mouches aux folâtres enfans; ils nous tuent pour s'amuser', quoted from *Œuvres complètes de Shakespeare, Traduites de l'anglais par Letourneur, Nouvelle édition* par F. Guizot (Paris: Ladvocat, 1821).

11. D. Kern Holoman, *The Société des Concerts du Conservatoire, 1827–1967* (Berkeley and Los Angeles: University of California Press, 2004).

12. *Memoirs*, chap. 46; *Mémoires* (ed. Bloom), 435; *The Memoirs* (trans. Cairns), 223.

13. Beate Angelika Kraus, 'Who is the Hero? The Early Reception of the *Eroica*', in Nancy November (ed.), *The Cambridge Companion to the Eroica Symphony* (Cambridge: Cambridge University Press, 2020), 192.

14. *Memoirs*, chap. 20; (ed. Bloom) *Mémoires*, 240; (trans. Cairns) *The Memoirs*, 82.

15. For comparison with Beethoven's Fifth and Sixth symphonies, see Rushton, *The Music of Berlioz*, 252–3.

16. Jean Mongrédien, *La Musique en France des Lumières au Romantisme 1789–1830* (Paris: Flammarion, 1986), on the symphony in that period, 258–66; cited (my translation), 259.
17. See Mark Evan Bonds, *The Beethoven Syndrome.*
18. 'On a profané Faust pour en faire un indigne mélodrame'. Letter to Nancy Berlioz, 1 November 1829. *CG* Vol. I, 213.
19. *CG* Vol. I, 217–18, letter tentatively dated 12 November 1828. Rochefoucauld's kindly rebuff is dated 19 November.
20. '. . . j'ai dans la tête depuis longtemps une *symphonie descriptive de Faust* qui fermente'. *CG* Vol. I, 232.
21. NBE 16, 191–3.
22. On Chateaubriand's effect on the programme, see Stephen Rodgers, *Form, Program, and Metaphor in the Music of Berlioz* (Cambridge: Cambridge University Press, 2009), 87.
23. See Hector Berlioz, *Roméo et Juliette*, ed. D. Kern Holoman, NBE Vol. 18 (Kassel: Bärenreiter, 1990), 2; Julian Rushton, *Berlioz: Roméo et Juliette* (Cambridge: Cambridge University Press, 1994), 87–8.
24. The poem was published in the *Revue des deux mondes* (1 August 1831); NBE Vol. 16, 171 (my prose translation).
25. On unrealized projects, see D. Kern Holoman, *Catalogue of the Works of Hector Berlioz*, NBE Vol. 25 (Kassel: Bärenreiter, 1987), 422–3. 'It's large-scale music that ruins me': *CG* Vol. II, 685.
26. For instance to Nancy Berlioz, 4 June 1827. *CG* Vol. I, 155.
27. Francesca Brittan, 'Fantastique', *CBE*, 119–20; Katherine Kolb, 'Fiction', *CBE*, 47–8. See also the discussion of Brittan's earlier work in Rodgers, *Form, Program, and Metaphor*, 87–9, and Francesca Brittan, *Music and Fantasy in the Age of Berlioz* (Cambridge: Cambridge University Press, 2017).
28. *Memoirs*, chap. 31.
29. For a full account of the premiere, see David Cairns, *Berlioz* Vol. I, 424–30.
30. Fétis's first review: *La Revue musicale* X (11 December 1830).
31. *Mémoires* (ed. Bloom), 411–13; *The Memoirs* (trans. Cairns), 206–9.
32. D. Kern Holoman, *The Creative Process in the Autograph Musical Documents of Hector Berlioz, c. 1818–1840* (Ann Arbor, MI: UMI Research Press, 1980), 262–82; NBE 16, 195–217.
33. D. Kern Holoman, *Berlioz* (London: Faber & Faber, 1989), 614–15.
34. Letter to Joseph d'Ortigue, 16 April 1846. *CG* Vol. III, 336–7. 'Inquiet' is gendered masculine, so it is a man who is anxious; a female would be 'inquiète'.

FIRST MOVEMENT

'Rêveries, passions'

In his letter to Ferrand of 16 April 1830 (see Chapter 1), Berlioz described the first movement as 'double, made up of a short adagio [*sic*], followed at once by an extended allegro'.[1] The Largo of sixty-three bars is not short, nor is it a mere introduction; lasting about four minutes, it is about a quarter of the whole movement. Its theme, the early Florian song, shares a motif with the *idée fixe* (see bracketed bars: 1 in Ex. 4.1 and 3 (cf. also 7) in Ex. 4.3).

Whereas most earlier symphonies, including Beethoven's, begin with an arresting gesture or motif, Berlioz's opens almost in a whisper: a two-bar introduction to the Florian song. The programme may imply Largo for reveries and Allegro for passions, but contrasting moods appear in both tempi. The programme, passing 'from a state of melancholy reverie, interrupted by bursts of unfounded happiness and stirrings of anger and jealousy, returning to tenderness, tears, and religious consolation' offers no precise guide as to where these feelings are located, and the listener is free to speculate.[2] The exultant climax, with the first entry of trumpets and cornets (410), may suggest 'unfounded happiness'. The movement originally ended *fortissimo* at bar 491. Its final bars no doubt represent 'religious consolation', although it is not known whether an access of piety suggested the quiet ending, or a decision to end quietly suggested suitable words for the programme.

Introductions do not usually include long melodies, though Beethoven's *Leonora* overtures (Nos. 2 and 3) form a precedent, being partly based on one of the opera's arias. The speed changes and dynamic surges and decays (with no 'heavy' brass or percussion) extend well beyond the normal language of a symphonic introduction (Table 4.1). Robert Schumann observed that the Largo has its own formal organization, although his description

4 First Movement: 'Rêveries, passions'

Example 4.1 The 'Florian song'. Largo, $\quad$ = 56

only partly corresponds to the facts; he identified 'two variations on a theme, with free *intermezzi* ", but his second variation is hard to recognize as such, and is defined in Table 4.1 as 'Transition'.[3]

Berlioz quite often defined tempo relationships proportionately. Cautioning the conductor not to slow down ('sans ralentir', 49) he suggests a whole bar of the Allegro is 'equivalent' to the Largo's crotchet, though strictly ♩ = 132 is faster than the Largo's ♩ = 56; Berlioz's 'équivaut' suggests that he was aware of the mathematical discrepancy.

Allegro agitato e appassionato assai ♩ = 132

Schumann noted that the Allegro differed from 'the traditional model', and mentioned 'frequent rough edges', presumably referring to its abrupt mood changes, while perceiving no real flaw in Berlioz's scheme. Despite his reservations, Schumann never condescended, nor did he suggest (as have later critics) that Berlioz did not understand 'correct' procedures; the overture *Waverley* (*c.* 1827) suffices to show that Berlioz could follow the 'traditional model' closely enough if he chose.

The 'traditional model' of a sonata form Allegro consists of (1) the exposition – two contrasted theme groups (P: primary and S: secondary), separated by a transition so that S is exposed in the dominant; (2) the middle section, usually called 'development', with various ideas in new harmonic situations; (3) a recapitulation in the tonic of both theme groups in the same order (P then S). There may follow closing material (peroration/coda), a feature of many Berlioz

49

Table 4.1 *First movement: Form of the Largo*

Bars 1–16	17–27	28–45	46–60	61–71
A	B	A' Variation:	C	Transition into
1–2: introduction	Episode 1	(2 bars longer)	Episode 2	the Allegro
C minor:	'Plus vite'	Eb to C minor:	Chord sequence over	Allegro from
Florian song	C major to 23	Florian song	Ab (=G♯)	bar 64
Bass Ab–G–C	Faster, then	Bass G–Ab	Resolves onto	Dominant
into bar 18	*rallentando*	into bar 46	A minor (vi)	preparation

A: The subdued woodwind on g′/g″ initiates the Florian song (muted violins), accompanied by silences and questing harmonies suggested by lines moving mainly by small intervals. As the tune rises, cellos in contrary motion open up a lower register. The bass pizzicato (12) unsettles temporary repose on an E♭ chord. Repeated bars (11–12) are harmonized by a full diminished seventh, resolved back to E♭, but the basses' D♭ requires resolution onto A♭. The melody resumes, but never reaches a cadence.

B: Basses (bowed) and cellos take A♭ down to G (16). Episode 1 is in C major, which comes suddenly: unstable, faster, and accelerating (20). Violins, now unmuted but *pp* and playing at the tip of the bow, rise and fall over more than two octaves, with excited fragments below; the second ascent (20) crescendos to *ff* with first and second violins – to left and right of the conductor – tangling together (23) as the music slows to Tempo I. The violin sextuplets, buoyant and hopeful, suddenly fade at the return to C minor (24), where woodwind and horn introduce a new melodic shape (heard just once) that steers the harmony to E♭ major. The texture solidifies (24–7) in wind triplets and string arpeggios, the last (27) slow enough to be played pizzicato.

A': The Florian song is at its original pitch despite being initially harmonized in E♭. The variation combines reverie with passion. The semiquaver sextuplets pass to woodwind, again covering over two octaves. E♭ is emphasized by the firm C♭ (29), but C minor cannot long be denied (32). The octave leaps (36) are now impressively answered by imitation, and the closing phrases are richly harmonized, touching chords of A♭, F minor, and by sequence D♭ (42) with preceding dominants.

Rather than preparing a cadence, however, the tune is again unfinished, dying amid uncertain string syncopations that clash with woodwind (44; A♭ against A♮). The upper strings' pizzicato (47) suggests a G chord, but the bass has reversed bars 16–17 and remains on A♭, held almost to the end of the Largo.

So far, this is as Schumann had it: theme, free intermezzo, variation. But bars 40–8 are not an episode but the dying away of the Florian song; what follows is not a second variation (Ex. 4.2).

C: The kaleidoscopic harmony (and enharmony) of Episode 2 unfolds over the pedal A♭, suggesting no definite outcome. A♭ is interpreted as fifth, root, and mediant of major and minor triads, outlined by flickering violins and gently articulated woodwind triplets (Ex. 4.2 shows the harmonies). Each melodic fragment on the horn has only a single response (52 partly inverts 50; 58 varies 56). The atmosphere is dusky, the mood pensive until the crescendo and harmonic breakthrough into C major, where the bass treats A♭ as G♯ to resolve to A minor. The dominant is finally reached by an orthodox progression (vi–IV–V), repeated with manic dynamic changes in the first Allegro bars; the cadence is completed (72) as the *idée fixe* begins.

Example 4.2 The Largo, bars 45–63: Harmonic outline

Allegros, and, for instance, Beethoven's Third Symphony (*Eroica*). Against this background the first-movement Allegro of *Symphonie fantastique* might seem wayward, and it has aroused differences of opinion (see Chapter 10). Table 4.2 is a simplified map of its tonal and thematic design, showing only keys well marked by themes or motives. As with the Largo, the sections overlap or merge, the end of one coincident with the outset of another.

Table 4.2 *First movement: Formal outline of the Allegro*

Exposition	Transition	72–167a repeated	Development	(Restatement of P)	Recap.	Episode	Recap.	Peroration	Coda
P 1, 2	(P)	S*	(P, S), athematic	(P), transition S	S	(P), solo oboe	P		
72–111	111–149	150–167a	166b–231	232–	322	358–409	410	439–91	491–525
P1 (72)		*begins like P1	S (191),	P (239–78),	S (322);			Animez;	Slowing;
P2 (119)			athematic (208)	S (311)	P2 (329–57)			P (451)	P
I	I–V/V	I–V/V	I (191)	V; iii (311)	I; to VI (A)	to V/I	I	(I)	Cadences

Note: P = Primary theme; P1 = *idée fixe*; S = Subsidiary theme; (P) = reference to motives from the *idée fixe*; I = the tonic (C); V = the dominant (G).

Berlioz decided to repeat the exposition only after writing out the score, adding two first-time bars (166–7); note that the second-time bars are also 166–7 in the New Berlioz Edition, whereas another modern edition (in the series Norton Critical Scores) numbers them 168–9; if consulting the latter while reading this, subtract two from higher bar numbers.[4] The first-time bars may sound perfunctory, returning to the almost unaccompanied *idée fixe*. However, this repetition allows us to assimilate material that is later developed and not literally recapitulated. In the second-time bars a sudden tremolo is made extra resonant by the second violins' open G-string, its shock value enhanced by our having previously heard the first-time ending (see Ex. 4.4, bar 166a).

The two points of recapitulation in Table 4.2 do not imply an orthodox sonata form, but the arrangement of keys and themes is, as it were, in dialogue with the 'traditional model'. Berlioz's aesthetic principle, that music should be 'free, sovereign', not governed by rules, permitted him to bring the *idée fixe* (P theme) in varied forms, notably at the recapitulation (410) where it is transformed from the artist's first association ('passionate, but also noble and reticent') into an exultant *tutti* at double speed (halved note values).

The *idée fixe* is a long and fluid melody, unusual for the P theme in sonata form (Ex. 4.3). Ostensibly serene, it is disturbed by multiple changes of speed and dynamics and by staccato interjections beneath, which are hardly an accompaniment; rather they suggest, as Charles Rosen says, 'a mimesis of the agitation in the poet's or musician's heart, an image of the passion that mounts as the melody proceeds'.[5]

The Allegro is marked by the signposts of sonata form, several 'correctly' placed: the transition to the dominant in the (repeated) exposition, with a cadence; development of P and S themes by fragmentation, modulation, and rhythmic alteration; recapitulation of both themes in the tonic; and a peroration/coda with the sense of an ending. Unlike Berlioz's usual Allegro procedure, the closing bars slow down, like the end of Beethoven's overture *Coriolan* but without its tragic implications.

Other elements depart from 'the traditional model' and also from the pattern established by the theorist Adolf Bernhard

53

Example 4.3 The *idée fixe* (P1) and its pendant (P2)

Marx, to whom we attribute the inaccurate, anachronistic, and offensive notion that P themes are 'strong' (masculine) and S themes gentle ('feminine') and lyrical, hence his use of the term *Gesangsperiode* (song section) for S themes; however, in this movement, the singing theme is P, the *idée fixe*. Undoubtedly many sonata forms before and after Berlioz (and Marx) are like

Example 4.4 The S theme, opening like the *idée fixe*

this, but others reverse this scheme, with S more assertive than P, and there are 'monothematic' movements (usually associated with Haydn but not confined to him) in which P and S themes start alike even if they proceed differently. This is what happens here (see Ex. 4.4), although S is not recapitulated in this form.

Schumann's 'traditional model' places the relative minor key in the development – the section traditionally understood as more adventurous, or stressed, with roving harmony and themes broken up to be reassembled in the recapitulation – and which often refers to minor keys in major-key movements. Such tendencies appear in the passage that leads to the tonic recapitulation of P, although (as Schumann noted) using E minor, iii, rather than the relative, A minor.

However, in the midst of what 'should' be development, after three silent bars, Berlioz re-establishes G major (232) and repeats the entire 'song' (*idée fixe*) in that key. Prior to this was a short development of the opening motive of the *idée fixe*; an exultant but premature return of S in the tonic, shorn of its opening reference to

P (191); and some athematic scrambling up and down chromatic scales (198–228) that might loosely refer to the first Largo episode (17–23) – perhaps an expression of jealous anger, soothed by the complete repetition of the *idée fixe*. Hence arises a question: is this G-major reprise, following three bars of silence and a seven-bar lead-in, the 'true' recapitulation of P, in the 'wrong' key? This idea gains plausibility as it is followed by a transition, partly in E minor and partly based on imitative entries of S (311), leading to the tonic reprise (410). So Berlioz's plan can be read as having recapitulations of themes P and S in the correct order, but with P in the wrong key; *or* (as in Table 4.2) the recapitulation is in the right key for both themes, but in reverse order. Neither procedure is impossible or unprecedented, though earlier examples may not have been familiar to Berlioz. I leave it to the reader to wonder: 'does it matter?'

Berlioz's sonata-type movements are usually less unorthodox, but he also, and unequivocally, reversed the thematic recapitulation in the first movement of *Harold en Italie*, where the practice could be justified, if justification were needed, by the development's concentration on the P theme. In *Symphonie fantastique* the issue would not be in doubt but for the reprise of the whole *idée fixe* prior to further development and its rhythmic transformation at the second point of recapitulation (see Table 4.2), quickly followed, as in *Harold en Italie*, by something new that prepares the ending.

Tracing the *Idée fixe*

The *idée fixe* (Ex. 4.3) is the main theme of the Allegro, but not of other movements; its scoring for violins and flute is also used for the main theme of the third movement. In the introduction to *Herminie* the first two phrases (violins) are followed by agitated material treated in imitation, its intervals altered to suit the harmony, as in the symphony's Allegro (from 166b and 361). A longer version of the tune appears in the middle of Herminie's second aria, played on wind instruments and sung. The text refers to the absent and unresponsive Tancredi: 'In vain I breathe my winged plea; I implore him; he does not hear me.'[6] The closing phrases of the melody were improved in the symphony: downward octaves (on 'implore') are replaced by a seventh, then a sixth (103–7). If Berlioz noticed the potential link to the Florian melody, he must have decided that the shared motif (bracketed in Ex. 4.1 and 4.3) was enough to show them as belonging together. More likely he cared less for such loose 'unification' of themes than for an effective close to his principal theme which, unlike the Florian melody, does reach a cadence.

The *idée fixe* shows Berlioz's predilection for unequal phrase lengths. Disregarding upbeats, the pattern is units of 8–7–4–4–4–5–8 bars (in Ex. 4.3 [1] marks the beginning of each unit). Rosen noted a loose overall symmetry: eight and an odd number at each end, 8–7 being reversed at the end as 5–8. The accompaniment multiplies beneath the sequential ascent (91–102); towards the cadence the texture is smoother, the harmony more chromatic.[7] The five-bar unit is an elongated version of four, and the final eight could be construed as 2 + 6. Further irregularities (from the point of view of the symmetry and unity considered desirable by early critics) are the longer half-bar upbeat to the final eight, and the late introduction of new rhythmic values, crotchet triplets. As for accompaniment, the gentle string syncopations of the *Herminie* aria are abandoned. Instead Berlioz leaves its first phrases (P1) unaccompanied, like some of the Florian song, and introduces rougher punctuation, an irregular stabbing (though *piano*) that intrudes on the elegance of the theme. Unequal phrase lengths had been a problem for French writers on music for decades, reflected in essays that, among other things, attack Gluck because the essence of melody should be the symmetrical 'period', the phrasing Berlioz called 'square' ('carré').[8] This adherence to the symmetrical period survived in the theoretical writings of Berlioz's teacher Antoine Reicha.[9] Berlioz's admiration for Gluck led him to build melodies expressively, resulting in phrase lengths that are often not at all 'carré'.

At this point (111) fiery passion breaks out (*con fuoco*): fast scales, *tutti* and *fortissimo* diminished sevenths, and a sequence of thirds plunging down and up, with ascending fourths in the bass, a passage that would surely have seemed *outré* to Berlioz's more conventional-minded listeners. It was a condition of romanticism that art may arouse astonishment, a notion rejected by earlier critics, such as one who accused 'Hayden' [*sic*] of wild modulations, seemingly intended to torment the listener.[10] Between two statements of this syntactically remarkable outburst (111, 125) comes a gentle pendant to the *idée fixe* (P2), a plea for calm that fails. The continuation (from 133) is no less disturbed, veering wildly towards F minor, A minor, and A♭ major, before getting a grip on the dominant of G (146).

The brief S theme is launched by a variant of the start of the *idée fixe*. The D♯ (Ex. 4.4, bar 2) means that the new motif takes off with E-minor harmony, hinting at later use of this key with this theme. Transposed up to start on D, the new motif (S) heads for the cadence into the first-time bar (166). The accompaniment resumes its stabbing figure, connecting it to P1, but off the beat.

The Movement's Centre and Ending

In the centre of the movement, the S motif and P2 take on independent life, detached from the *idée fixe*. Reveries and passions continue to alternate; while there is no evidence that Berlioz thought this way, his later handling of the *idée fixe* may suggest the protagonist invoking the beloved's image. The complete statement in G (239–78) is preceded by wildly surging chromatic scales that end, as if astonished, on an A-major chord (first inversion, 228), followed by a measured silence and a soft horn note, as if to say 'listen!' This reprise is developmental only in its accompaniment, continuous though still disturbed, with off-beat basses and a viola tremolo to cement a brittle texture stretching over four octaves.

Otherwise, until the two recapitulation points (see Table 4.2), and between them, the music is more conventionally developmental. Immediately after the exposition repeat, the opening bars of the *idée fixe* are reshaped (a fifth replaces a rising sixth). The first bar loses its dotted rhythm (179) and moves steadily up until the basses reach G two octaves above their point of departure. Four bars reiterating a dominant seventh introduce the premature tonic reprise of 'S' (191). Then come the athematic chromatics and the reprise in G. The *idée fixe* cadences as before (278), but the bass, moving slowly in minims, does not conform, having only reached the mediant, B. It then becomes the principal voice and questions G major by its B♭, bringing tonal uncertainty even though the violins retain their D. Uncertainty grows when (284) the violins rise through D♯ and return through E♭, but a revival of energy brings back G major (291). Without reference to themes P or S, the next bars seem almost optimistic, but if so the mood is shattered at the top of the crescendo (304), the first full wind chord for some time, by a sequence of all three possible diminished sevenths. The last resolves onto E minor for a short fugal imitation on S, building towards its second tonic reprise (in Table 4.2, point 1 of the recapitulation, 322).

This apparent recovery of harmonic and thematic stability cannot endure. At a cadence (329), woodwind intone a wistful reminiscence of P2, taken over by violins. Timpani, silent since the *fortissimo* 102 bars earlier, add an ominous roll (sponge-headed sticks). P2 is developed, descending through the string sections, each marked *canto*. Between the violas and basses, an extension (349–51) darkens the atmosphere, referring to C minor (by E♭, A♭, even D♭); the basses' *canto* expands the falling fifth, C♯ replacing the expected D. P2 has again failed to restore calm, and its wistful quality now becomes foreboding, though the resulting A major at first appears peaceful. Imitations (from 364), reminiscent of the *Herminie* introduction, follow the ascending sixth of the *idée fixe* with rising or falling semitones, and after two bars the imitation is compressed, dropping the upbeat quaver (from 370).

That was probably how the passage was first written. Later Berlioz added its most eloquent feature: the oboe solo starting from the *a tempo* (358) and seeming to surf harmonies already prescribed by the strings. In its later stages (380–92), this recalls the intervals of the astonishing progression that preceded the S material in the exposition (133–8). Tom S. Wotton was surely mistaken to conclude from the 1846 letter from Prague that Berlioz considered the oboe solo to be a version of the *idée fixe*; its urgent but insecure ascent is different in rhythm, phrasing, and intervals.[11] Steadily rising pitches, with violins joining the motivic play, form a prolonged crescendo culminating on the dominant (406) and the explosion of joy that marks the recapitulation of the *idée fixe*, assisted by cornets 'à pistons' (chromatic), trumpets (confined to the natural harmonic series), and piccolo.

Throughout the symphony, Berlioz varied the harmonization of the *idée fixe*. The small changes in the central reprise may pass unnoticed, but the recapitulation in halved values with syncopations requires a more compressed harmonic scheme. The waltz and third movement require other changes; curiously, the most conventional harmonization is that of the vulgar jig in the finale.[12] At the first-movement recapitulation the exuberant, even brash, version could suggest the lover's overconfidence (he will be disappointed). Berlioz undermines the mood first by going higher; where the theme in the exposition started its descent, the flute reaches g''' three times (429–36) and the violins reach a tone higher.

The continuation breaks into new territory at *animez* (439), with C major undermined by a first-inversion chord of B, the moment marked by the departure of timpani and brass. This moment would be startling even if it remained *fortissimo*. The dynamic drop, adding to the harmonic shock, is a springboard for somewhat desperate attempts to restore confidence. The bass pizzicato may seem ominous, as in the Largo, but the mood remains mercurial. Each harmonically unstable acceleration is followed by slower imitative passages based on the opening of the *idée fixe*. These start in C major but the first drifts via C minor onto D♭ (bassoon), then breaks back into the *più animato* (461). The second crescendo is completed with furious offbeat accents and a short passage (487–90) reminiscent of the first bars of the Allegro that precede the exposition of the *idée fixe*.

The movement originally ended with a full C-major chord (491), pitched high and with a return of trumpets, cornets, and timpani. Perhaps recalling that any optimism was misplaced, Berlioz added a coda to the coda. The oboe line (491–500), hardly a melody, is heard above the first part of the *idée fixe*, in equal crotchets, so without its springing dotted rhythm; then comes a lingering memory (500), mostly unaccompanied, as if drained of hope. The drawn-out final chords, a hymn-like 'Amen', are simple in themselves, but they contain the G–A♭–G–A♮–G of the *idée fixe*. Berlioz used a similar alternation of tonic and other chords for the 'Amen' at the close of his Requiem. This allusion to 'religious consolation' is another aspect of the protagonist's mood swings, which turn to something more creative at the conclusion of the sequel, *Lélio*.

***

To summarize: the first movement is unconventional: in the length of the Largo and, in the Allegro, its nonconformity to standard sonata forms, notwithstanding the repeated exposition with modulation to the dominant, many developmental activities, and recapitulation of themes in the tonic. The main departure from norms is the central repeat of the whole *idée fixe*, an area in sonata forms where tonal stability is usually avoided. The identification of the coda's beginning could be disputed, but taking the G-major *idée fixe* as recapitulation places the coda at its C-major transformation (410); as the movement's main climax, this is surely integral to the sonata-form action despite its interruption thirty bars on. In any case, it would be rash to conclude that the departures from the norm were unintentional or clumsy. What they do show is that Berlioz, who might not have composed a symphony at all but for the impact of Beethoven, nevertheless did not consider himself strictly bound by precedent; instead, he took the liberty of extending the symphony's bounds and interpreting its formal practices in his own way (see also Chapter 10). His writings on Beethoven are not much concerned with form, but both composers would have agreed that mere formalism should never restrict an artist's imagination. Berlioz often denounced composers and writers on music who were over-respectful of precedent and routine, and he might have approved the pillorying of formalist attitudes in an early novel by George Bernard Shaw (*Love among the Artists*, 1881): the fictional composer observes critics discussing why his work 'ought not to have been written' (compare Le Sueur on Beethoven's Fifth); 'my first subject, my second subject, my working out, and the rest of the childishness that could be taught to a poodle'. A real composer, Elliott Carter, glimpsed the future in the first movement of *Symphonie fantastique* because it hints at a 'stream of consciousness' such as he also found in Debussy.[13]

Revisions

Having overwritten, Berlioz tended to cut and jettison part of his first version, so what was performed in 1830 cannot be reconstructed. The symphony as we know it was essentially premiered in 1832. Two large cuts have been identified, possibly amounting to *c*. 20 per cent of the 1830 Allegro. Of these, a few fragments survive, including another iteration of theme S in its exposition form, starting with two bars of the *idée fixe*. A large cut came between bars 274 and 312; the fragment shows an inexplicable double-bar, as if for a repeat, with G major implied, although a return to the G-major version of the *idée fixe* (239) seems highly unlikely. Other alterations are on 'collettes' (cut-off pages or scraps of music paper pasted into the autograph) under which original thoughts can sometimes be discerned.[14] There is, however, little doubt that Berlioz's alterations were improvements in design, as was usually the case with him, whether shortening the music, as here, or as in the second movement, actually making it longer.

Notes

1. See Chapter 1, n. 12.
2. NBE 16, 167–70.
3. Robert Schumann, 'A Symphony by Berlioz', *Neue Zeitschrift für Musik*, July–August 1835. Citations are from the translation in Ian Bent (ed.), *Music Analysis in the Nineteenth Century II: Hermeneutic Approaches* (Cambridge: Cambridge University Press, 1994), 161–94; cited 173. There is another complete translation in Cone, *Berlioz: Fantastic Symphony*, 215–48.
4. New Berlioz Edition Vol. 16; the Norton Critical score is included in Cone, *Fantastic Symphony*.
5. Charles Rosen, *The Romantic Generation* (London: HarperCollins, 1996), 546–50; cited, 547.
6. 'J'exhale en vain ma plainte fugitive. Je l'implore, il ne m'entend pas'. Hector Berlioz, *Prix de Rome Works*, ed. David Gilbert, NBE 6 (Kassel: Bärenreiter, 1998), 86–7.
7. Rosen, *The Romantic Generation*, 547–9.
8. For instance in Jean-François Marmontel's polemical 'Essai sur les Révolutions de la Musique en France' (1777), reprinted with commentary in G.M. Leblond (1781), *Mémoires pour servir à l'histoire*

de la révolution opérée dans la musique par M. le Chevalier Gluck, reproduced in François Lesure (ed.), *Querelle des Gluckistes et des Piccinnistes* (Geneva: Minkoff, 1984), Vol. I, 153–190; see p. 169.

9. Antoine Reicha, *Traité de mélodie* (Paris: Antoine Reicha, 1814).

10. Pierre-Louis Ginguené, *Mélophile à l'homme de lettres chargé de la rédaction des articles de l'Opéra*, reprinted in Lesure (ed.), *Querelle des Gluckistes et des Piccinnistes*, Vol. II, 595–621; see p. 605.

11. The letter is cited in Chapter 3, note 34; also see Tom S. Wotton, *Berlioz: Four Works*, in the series The Musical Pilgrim (London: Oxford University Press, 1929), 15, where he mistakenly translates 'on' as 'she' despite the masculine-gendered adjective that follows.

12. The harmonic changes are superimposed in Julian Rushton, *The Musical Language of Berlioz* (Cambridge: Cambridge University Press, 1983), 99–102.

13. Elliott Carter, *Collected Essays and Lectures, 1937–1995*, ed. Jonathan W. Bernard (University of Rochester Press, 1997), 131.

14. See NBE Vol. 16, 195–217; D. Kern Holoman, *The Creative Process in the Autograph Musical Documents of Hector Berlioz*, 262–82.

5

SECOND MOVEMENT

'*Un bal*'

A symphonic waltz was unusual for 1830, perhaps unprecedented, but early audiences, who paid relatively little attention to symphonies, probably accepted it without complaint. It replaces the faster scherzos in Beethoven's symphonies without reverting to the classical minuet; curiously, Berlioz used these only for supernatural evocations, the 'Queen Mab' scherzo in *Roméo et Juliette*, and Mephistopheles summoning fiery spirits ('Menuet des follets') in *La Damnation de Faust*.

As a relief from the emotional struggles of the first movement, 'Un bal' is the least intense part of the symphony. It represents a social event that the protagonist attends and where, the programme tells us, as in the country, 'the beloved image comes to him and troubles his soul'. The 1830 programme does not suggest she herself is at the ball. The revised programme has her there, perhaps giving her lover grounds for hope; so after we hear the *idée fixe* the whirling dance resumes to reach an exuberant conclusion. Yet what the lover takes as interest in him could have been a passing attraction under the influence of dance-music, or merely politeness; realization of this leads to a surge of jealousy in the third movement.

The overall form is almost strophic (Table 5.1). After the short introduction, each of the four sections begins in the same way, with the tune (Ex. 5.1) only a little varied except in its orchestral colouring. Its fourth iteration is abbreviated, merging into the coda, which is marked *animez* (as in the first movement). The *idée fixe* appears in full as an episode, in a key (F) only indirectly related to the tonic; it reappears briefly as a reminiscence within the coda, now reconciled to the key of A.

The waltz theme (Ex. 5.1) is carefully phrased, with a footnote to explain a straight line between notes (43, 51); combined with a slur,

Table 5.1 *Form of 'Un bal'*

1–36	37	94	121	176	233	256
Introduction	Waltz (1)	Waltz (2)	Episode	Waltz (3)	Waltz (4)	Coda
Includes X motif	Extension;	Tonal dissolve:	*Idée fixe*	Extension;		Reminiscence
	X from 54	*idée fixe.*		X from 191		of *idée fixe*
A (minor to major)	A	A–F; transition	F: transition	A	A	320: *con fuoco*

Example 5.1 'Un bal', the waltz theme ($\downarrow$. = 60)

this implies string *portamento* (sliding; so it is omitted when the wind play the theme).

The movement is lightly scored. Horns are the only brass; there is only one oboe and no bassoons. To get the pitches he wanted, Berlioz required four horns – a pair in E and a pair in C – and on natural horns only a few notes require hand-stopping, but at this dynamic level changes in timbre should not be noticeable.

In the interests of balance and glitter Berlioz wanted 'at least two' harps on each part. The opening harmony, A minor, follows the soft C-major ending of the first movement. Beneath a *tremolo*, lower strings describe a motivic shape unrelated to the waltz tune ('X' in Table 5.1). Four versions of it, swelling to an offbeat *sf* and dying back, change the harmony to F major, at which point the harps reach two octaves above the violins. The harmony is unsettled, anticipatory: F via a diminished triad becomes F♯ minor, two chords remote in the harmonic spectrum but connected by sharing the mediant (A). As after the first-movement double bar, the harmonies shift by semitones rather than thirds or fifths. For this reason, and without implying any aesthetic weakness (rather the contrary), Leonard B. Meyer discusses the passage under the rubric 'weakening of shape'.[1] The sequence of harmonies runs: a–F–diminished–f♯–F♯; this is repeated a tone higher (from 13), ending enharmonically on A♭. By now we are far removed from the tonic, but as the excitement grows, a dominant 6–4 is reached via two more diminished sevenths (30); harps join woodwind in glittering scales. Three bars of 'till ready' (36–8) prepare the waltz tune. This emergence of a brilliantly lit ballroom from a tonal mist anticipates *La Valse* by Maurice Ravel (not among Berlioz's warmest admirers).

The first statement of the waltz tune (37) is mostly on strings with woodwind touches. The offbeat accompaniment continues for sixteen bars; for this formal dance Berlioz, despite his predilection for asymmetry, resorts to four-bar phrases. Then (54) the lower strings join the harps (pizzicato); the bass figure resembles the introduction (X). The violins resume with two nearly identical five-bar phrases; as Berlioz pointed out, twice five is no less symmetrical than twice four.[2] These phrases are separated by one bar (61) and so disturb the regularity of the dance. The music grows more frenzied, less overtly tuneful, with pitches foreign to A major: D♯s, then F♮ (*sf*, basses, 76), and C♮ (woodwind, 78–85). These are quickly resolved to E and B, and the firm bass E and re-entry of the harps restore order. The music returns gently to the waltz (94), now with a perky offbeat accompaniment from harps and woodwind.

The bars marked '*rallent[ando]*' in the first statement (49–50) are now 'sans retenir', pushing ahead (106) to concentrate on a motif in dialogue between violins and wind. This suddenly lurches from an E chord (115) to F♮; cellos slither over two octaves, and the dominant of F prepares the *idée fixe* on flute and oboe (121). For its second phrase the oboe is replaced by clarinet (129), starting in unison with the flute but soon compelled to go an octave lower, a favourite doubling for Berlioz (continuing in unison would be too shrill). Here, perhaps, the protagonist catches a glimpse of his beloved, even meets her, dances with her ... but with a trace of angst, as the accompaniment below a *tremolo* recalls the staccato bass interjections of the first movement, offbeat and somewhat unnerving although *pianissimo*.

A short transition (from 160) offers a little harmonic and textural uncertainty, with an athematic exchange between wind and strings. The music is stabilized by the held E (third horn); the other horns join as the wind–string dialogue wavers between upper neighbours, as in the *idée fixe* (here F♯ and F♮). The longer the E continues the more it sounds like a dominant; the waltz duly resumes in the tonic (176) with a strikingly original string texture, the tune doubled in second violins, violas an octave below, and cellos an octave below the violas. Textural security is provided by a double-bass tonic pedal, pizzicato; and to all this are added a wind figure (with cornet if used) and harp triplets. Berlioz's orchestral imagination is here at its most genial. When the wind appropriate the tune (205), the strings exchange pizzicato arpeggios, loosely related to the X motif of the introduction. The C♮–B motif (215, second violins) is almost buried by interlocking wind and first violins. A short crescendo halts at the subdominant (D) chord (227; cf. bar 90).

In the following bars the piccolo makes its second appearance in the symphony; after a bar of silent anticipation it joins in the last full statement of the waltz tune (233), in woodwind over three octaves, as previously with the strings. The waltz accompaniment (pizzicato) is pitted against horn harmonies, with offbeat accentuation. At bar 256, Berlioz writes *animez*, with new motivic shapes, mainly scalar: up in the woodwind, down in the strings. Such animation is characteristic of his codas, of which this is a relatively long example. Its opening is repeated after sixteen bars (272) with added harps, and the waltz grows more frenetic after a further sixteen, with cross-beat phrasing in the melody as it approaches a *fortissimo*. But then comes an abrupt halt: a lone clarinet recalls the *idée fixe*, minimally harmonized (flute and horn). The *idée fixe* begins in an unprepared subdominant, alien from its glittering surroundings, but as a natural result its second phrase, ushered in by harps, returns to the tonic (cf. Ex. 4.3). The last bars of this reminiscence are newly minted, adding the second clarinet – another characteristically delicate touch, as it moves on its own, sounding E–D to imply a dominant seventh, in the husky 'throat' register that separates the rich low notes from the cantabile register of the first clarinet.

The rest of the orchestra breaks, *con fuoco*, into this moment of reverie, but with an air of social enjoyment rather than passion. The solid A major still alludes to notes borrowed from the parallel minor, turning to full-blooded chords of C and F (333–4), which are quickly brushed aside; Berlioz glories in such enhancement of closing bars in other works, for instance the overtures *Le Roi Lear* and *Le Corsaire*. A further *animez* (338) brings back the waltz tune's first bars in *stretto*. The *idée fixe* is banished; the beloved, real or imaginary, is no longer with the protagonist, or when (in the later version of the programme) the movement is part of his dream, she has disappeared, thoughts of her temporarily extinguished by the virtual orgy of the coda.

Revision

This coda was shorter in 1830; Berlioz increased its length and brilliance during his time in Italy. The version of the movement heard in 1830 is not extant, and the surviving autograph is on Italian music paper, with the note Berlioz wrote to Habeneck before setting off to Paris, intending to kill his fiancée and then himself.[3] At over 100 bars, the coda is more than a quarter of the movement. Even without the cornet (which adds counterpoint and fanfares) the city-life quality of the movement is abundantly clear, in contrast to the country scene that follows. The material was worth extending; there is no sense of redundancy, and the decisive signing off is a frank invitation to applause.

The main revision after 1831 was the string counterpoint, using motives from the waltz, that Berlioz added as counterpoint to the *idée fixe* from its second phrase (128–56; see Ex. 5.2, from bar 128). This does not appear in Liszt's transcription as the change was made well over a decade later, and after several performances; it was written around the time of publication, between the printing of an 'advance' copy and the definitive version of the full score.[4] But although, as Temperley observes, it is hard to see when composition ends and revision begins, it is remarkable that Berlioz hit on this felicitous idea so long after the initial impulse to compose, and revise, such an important work.[5]

Berlioz also added a cornet solo to the waltz, for which the only source is the autograph. If, as seems likely, it was composed for the virtuoso Jean-Baptiste Arban (born 1825), it must have been written into the MS after publication of the full score. Temperley suggests that it could have been added for a special occasion, and relegates it to an appendix in the New Berlioz Edition.[6] The cornet

69

Example 5.2 'Un bal', version of the *idée fixe*

enters briefly at the climax of the introduction, then rests until bar 106; later it adds new but simple counterpoints, with no effect on the musical structure, unless one counts as a disturbance the added arpeggio on the subdominant (227), after which it doubles the waltz tune. The solo is usually omitted, although its garishness enhances the contrast with the following Adagio.

Notes

1. Leonard B. Meyer, *Emotion and Meaning in Music* (Chicago: University of Chicago Press, 1956), 180–1.
2. 'Strauss, son orchestra, ses valses. – De l'avenir du rhythme', *Journal des débats* (10 November 1837). Trans. Julian Rushton, 'Johann Strauss and the Future of Rhythm', *Berlioz Society Bulletin* 212 (January 2021), 43–53.

3. Berlioz, *Memoirs*, chap. 34.
4. Holoman, *The Creative Process*, 280–2, including a facsimile of Berlioz's sketch for the passage.
5. NBE 16, IX.
6. NBE 16, pp. XIV, 197. The score in Cone, *Berlioz.Fantastic Symphony*, has the cornet part in small notes.

THIRD MOVEMENT

'Scène aux champs'

Like a picture in a gallery, the Adagio proper is enclosed by a frame (see Table 6.1). If it started at bar 20, with its principal theme, and ended at bar 175, perhaps with a chord rather than a single cello note, it would seem complete. The framing music appears nowhere else, and in character it is neither introduction nor coda; it is further separated from the rest by its instrumentation. The closing section is not mentioned in early versions of the programme, but this need not imply that it was a late addition.

The Adagio proper shows an affinity to Beethoven's reverie 'Scene by the brook' (*Pastoral Symphony*), but the resemblance is more homage than imitation and Berlioz's movement represents a range of emotions. Raymond Monelle observes that the comparison 'reveals the great aesthetic distance between these two composers', connecting this difference to Schiller's conception of 'naïve' and 'sentimental' artists because 'Berlioz is always concerned with expressing feelings, portrayal, narrative, evocation'.[1] But Beethoven, hardly a naïve composer, is also concerned with feelings; his first movement is 'Happiness aroused on arriving in the country'. True, Beethoven's feelings seem uncomplicated by yearning for a distant beloved, and the last three movements of the *Pastoral* are more imitative than introspective. Schumann associated the two composers: as against Haydn and Mozart, 'Berlioz belongs more to those Beethovenian characters whose artistic development conforms exactly to the course of their lives, such that for each fresh impetus in the former a corresponding new phase is initiated in the latter'.[2]

Another point of contrast is that Beethoven's scene is 'by the brook', whereas Berlioz's programme makes no reference to running water, despite the second stanza of Florian's poem, which recalls seeing the beloved's reflection in a stream. Nor was

Table 6.1 *Form of 'Scène aux champs' (Adagio ♩= 84)*

1–19	20–66	67–86	87–112
Frame			**Crisis**
Ranz, echoed	20–47 Theme P exposition 48–67 transition (to dominant)	67–77 Theme P with birdsong 77–87 interruption; transition (to subdominant)	87–99 *idée fixe*, introduced by bass motif 100–12 *animez* Interruption, with bass motif, then athematic; crisis
F	F → C (V)	C—Bb (IV)	Bb—> ?V/F

113–30	131–49	150–74	175–99
Recovery		**Coda**	**Frame**
117 Theme P varied, added counterpoint	Theme P with counterpoint lesser crisis and recovery	*idée fixe* with birdsong	Ranz, no echo Distant thunder
F	C (V)	F	F

Berlioz's isolation quite like the German poet Eichendorff's *Waldeinsamkeit*: forest loneliness, memorably evoked by Schumann in his song cycle (*Liederkreis*, Op. 39). The original scene of Berlioz's 'spleen' is not the river Isère but the plain near La Côte-Saint-André; his family owned a farm as well as the handsome town house that is now the Berlioz museum. When he again became 'prey' to spleen in Italy Berlioz recalled how it felt when aged sixteen, writing in chapter 40 of his memoirs: '*I was in anguish, slumping down, groaning* ... *convulsively ripping up fistfuls of grass and harmless daisies* ... *struggling against absence, against this terrible isolation.*'[3]

Introducing sounds of the country into serious music (here rustling leaves, birdsong, thunder, a cow-call) was discussed by Berlioz in his article 'On musical imitation' (1837).[4] Literal imitation, he suggests, ranges from the trivial to the sublime, but more important is imitation of *feelings* that suggest no direct musical analogue and can only be imitated metaphorically, by movement, harmony, texture, or colour. Music cannot convey *precisely* what it is that gives rise to feelings in the listener, and Berlioz made this point in his defence of expressive instrumental music.[5] Hence he accepted onomatopoeia so long as it was not indulged in for its own sake. Beethoven's storm is associated with the terror of country people; it breaks up their merrymaking, and in the finale they offer thanks for the storm's passing. Berlioz could also invoke Gluck's operas to justify musical imitation: the Elysian scene in *Orphée*, the enchanted garden in *Armide*, and the storm that opens *Iphigénie en Tauride*, all of which mirror the emotions of the principal characters. The latter opera was among Berlioz's first operatic experiences; as the storm abates, Iphigenia sings 'The storm abates, but, alas, it still rages in my heart.'

Direct imitation of birdsong had contributed to European music for centuries. Unlike Beethoven in the coda to 'Scene by the brook', Berlioz does not identify birdsong in this movement, but it is implied (he had labelled it in the prelude to his 1827 cantata, *Orphée*). From bar 67 a rustling string turn is echoed by a birdlike figure in the higher woodwind, reminiscent of Beethoven's flute which is a poor imitation of a nightingale, whereas his quail and cuckoo are unmistakable. In Berlioz's movement the rhythm

Example 6.1 The *ranz des vaches*

characteristic of a quail appears on instruments in octaves (69–77) rather than Beethoven's more literal high oboe, and Berlioz integrates this rhythm into the orchestral texture rather than having it standing out, like Beethoven's birds, as a separate section. The quail rhythm is already present within the main theme (see Ex. 6.2, brackets beneath bars 24 and 26). Describing the peaceful scene of his first attack of spleen, Berlioz mentions 'the amorous quail calling their mates'.

The Frame: *Ranz des Vaches*

The cor anglais, neither English nor a horn but an alto oboe, is the frame's principal voice; it is not used elsewhere. At the opening, its five phrases (Ex. 6.1) are imitated by an offstage oboe, an octave higher. Berlioz calls this solo a *ranz des vaches* (cow-call), but chooses not to use the obvious substitute for an alphorn, which would be the open notes of an orchestral horn; moreover, he does not confine himself to the notes likely to be available on such an instrument. Perhaps he did not wish to be accused of imitating Beethoven; the horn solo that opens the finale of the *Pastoral* Symphony is strikingly similar to a Swiss alphorn motif quoted

75

by Monelle.[6] Berlioz's choice of instrument was possibly influenced by Rossini, as his *ranz des vaches* (after the storm in the overture to *Guillaume Tell*), which Berlioz called 'delightful' in a review of 1834, is also for cor anglais, and is echoed an octave higher (but by a flute).[7] Rossini's melody is more flowing than a typical cow-call, and breaks into trills; but its opening motif could be played on a natural horn without recourse to hand-stopping. So might Berlioz's first phrase, except its last note (which would need slight flattening of the seventh harmonic to be in tune).

Berlioz knew of such functional music. His chorus of shepherds, one of the surviving numbers of *Les Francs-juges*, is 'a free adaptation of the Gruyère Ranz des Vaches (Ranz Fribourgeois)'; Berlioz could have heard the different adaptation in Grétry's *Guillaume Tell* when it was revived (1828), or read Grétry's probable source, Rousseau's *Dictionnaire de musique*, where it is headed 'cornemuse' (bagpipe).[8] In *Les Francs-juges* orchestral horns are echoed by offstage horns on the left, which are echoed in turn by clarinets on the right; the echoes at one-bar intervals overlap, and are all at the same pitch. In 'Scène aux champs' Berlioz's oboe does not *echo* the cor anglais, as it is an octave higher. It *responds* from a distance (the second oboe is not required for 'Un bal', so the player has ample time to go 'derrière la scène'). In his treatise, Berlioz compared the exchange to a pastoral dialogue, a young man's voice answering that of a girl ('la voix d'un adolescent répondant à celle d'une fille'), although it is the metaphorical male (cor anglais) who initiates the dialogue.[9] He refers to heartbreaking desolation when the cor anglais receives no oboe answer at the close, adding that no other instrument could arouse such an intense response from the listener. Berlioz might have lighted on the unique timbre of the cor anglais anyway, without thinking of Rossini; before the premiere of *Guillaume Tell* he had used it in the *Huit Scènes de Faust*. Marguerite's 'Romance', in which the haunting melody is introduced by the cor anglais, expresses her sense of loss; she has been deserted by her lover, Faust, whereas the symphony's protagonist is convinced *she* does not love him . . .

As for the style of Berlioz's *ranz des vaches*, this is a symphony, not an opera like *Les Francs-juges* or *Guillaume Tell*. It seems Berlioz felt a more stylized music was appropriate to convey the *impression* of a functional cow-call despite being nothing of the kind (Ex. 6.1, written at sounding pitch; the score is written a fifth higher). The tune is probably his own invention as, unlike the *Francs-juges* example, no model has been identified.[10] Wagner did something similar, also using cor anglais, in Act III of *Tristan und Isolde*; a simple opening, plausible on the shepherd's instrument, becomes improbably chromatic.

The second, third, and fourth phrases of Berlioz's *ranz des vaches* introduce pitches unavailable on a simple instrument without fingerholes, before returning to diatonicism in the fifth phrase. The melody is carefully structured; the second and fourth phrases imitate the rhythm of the first and third. Phrase 1 uses the pentatonic set common in much folk music: F G A C D, ending on D, as if modally, rather than F, on which it began. Phrase 2 uses only four pitches, with no D, and the A is flattened. Phrase 3 includes half a chromatic scale (G to C); the B♮ hints at the Lydian mode Berlioz had used in Marguerite's ballad 'Le Roi de Thulé' (*Huit Scènes de Faust*). Phrase 4 clearly suggests F *minor*; phrase 5 returns to diatonic F major, rounding off the melody with four notes from the first phrase (lacking G), and a new melodic shape and rhythm. When the oboe repeats the second and third phrases, the cor anglais – improbably for a cowherd – adds counterpoint. The two voices overlap prettily in the fifth phrase, at a distance of three quavers – a mini-canon rather than an echo. Each instrument hold its last note into bar 20; the oboist has twenty-seven long bars in which to rejoin the orchestra.

Berlioz's *ranz* is 'art music', with dynamics, accents, and slurs carefully notated, and using ten different pitches from the possible twelve, one of them appearing enharmonically as A♭ and G♯. The only other sounds at first are divided violas, *tremolo*, foreshadowing thunder at the close. There the cor anglais repeats all five phrases, but not its counterpoint, for no oboe is heard; instead, we hear distant thunder on four timpani tuned to different pitches.

The Main Theme of the Adagio

The main theme is taken from the 'Gratias agimus' of the *Messe solennelle*, a text that offers thanks to God but continues with a prayer for mercy ('miserere nobis'). Perhaps Berlioz in his better moods ('positive spleen') recalled this thanksgiving, not unmixed with anxiety, as suitable music for a pastoral reverie. Apart from the key (F rather than E), the main theme (Ex. 6.2) is reproduced almost exactly, as is its second iteration, doubled in thirds (from 33). The only change is in the fifth and seventh bars; the last two notes, originally even semiquavers, now anticipate the 'quail rhythm'. In the Mass, the melody is unaccompanied, without even the symphony's minimal punctuation of pizzicato lower strings. This lovely inspiration fits a pastoral atmosphere so well that one is tempted to think Berlioz conceived the 'Gratias' as a pastoral; some of the Mass was composed at La Côte-Saint-André, within a short distance of his first fit of 'mal de l'isolement'.

In the 'Gratias' the violins are doubled by clarinets. In the symphony, perhaps significantly, Berlioz used the flute–violin doubling that first introduced the *idée fixe*. He added dynamic

Example 6.2 'Scène aux champs', main theme

markings, there being none in the Mass other than *piano*; these barely disturb the atmosphere of tranquillity. While the theme is repeated in thirds, Berlioz added a sort of descant marked ***ppp*** (clarinet), starting with an augmentation of the first four notes of the melody (each note lasts a whole bar). From bar 41 the upper part (first violins, first flute) ceases to double the theme in thirds and takes over the descant. Meanwhile, casting the only shadow on this harmonious combination, a horn plays a melancholy rising and falling figure: C–Db–C (36, repeated two bars later with clarinet), then repeated but with a whole tone (C–D–C, 40), an unmistakable allusion to the *idée fixe*.

The *Idée fixe*

The programme is simple. The protagonist feels 'a new hopeful-ness' on leaving town, but despite enjoying the calm, despite his isolation, his hopes are mingled with foreboding and an access of jealousy. It is easy enough to read these feelings into music with episodes of surprising violence for an Adagio; this is perhaps the closest Berlioz came to representing those attacks of spleen in which distance from human contact induced extreme mood swings.

When the *idée fixe* appears it is disturbed, even assaulted, by a furious passage for strings (Ex. 6.3). This is not athematic, and nor is it an accompaniment. The bracketed motif in Ex. 6.3 is not new, having appeared at the close of the main theme (compare bar 87 in Ex. 6.3 with bar 47 in Ex. 6.4). This marks a personal crisis of a kind missing from the Andante of Beethoven's *Pastoral*. The desolation at the close is 'real' within Berlioz's plot, the *ranz* and thunder being diegetic, like a song performed in a film. It also serves as a metaphor for the protagonist's loneliness and growing despair, which led, in the original programme, to his attempted suicide.

At its main appearance in this movement, the *idée fixe* is not its original ardent self, nor does it lilt as in 'Un Bal' to fit easily with the waltz metre. This adaptation to a compound metre looks distorted on the page, because the note values and rhyth-mic proportions are almost exactly those of the first-movement exposition. The string interventions that perhaps represent the protagonist's jealousy conform to the metre, but what were

Example 6.3 'Scène aux champs', *idée fixe*

Example 6.4 'Scène aux champs', new motif with 'quail' rhythm

strong beats in the *idée fixe* now appear on weak parts of the bar and vice versa (these are marked * in Ex. 6.3).

Form of the Adagio

Adolf Bernhard Marx 'maintained that by "looking inward" when writing "a tranquil Adagio" a composer might hope to 'receive an answer to the question "Who am I?"'[11] Berlioz's far-from-tranquil

Adagio reminds us that he was not a tranquil person. Following the double exposition of the main theme, he introduces a more urgent figure of repeated notes (48) and a partly chromatic sighing figure on woodwind, redeploying the quail rhythm to form a new motive (Ex. 6.4). It is soon shorn of its final quaver, and when immediately repeated (60–3) it challenges the 6/8 metre (twice three quavers) by bars sounding as three times two quavers as if in 3/4 (Berlioz beamed the passage as 6/8 to assist the performers). The quail rhythm uses new intervals in a crescendo assisted by repeated wind semiquavers. Bar 59 resolves a diminished seventh onto A minor, and the inexorable bass (from 60) leads to a cadence in that key, relative of the dominant more intense than the relative to the tonic, which would be D minor (as with the E rather than A minor in the first movement).

This is only a brief upheaval; tranquillity is restored by three transitional bars that steer towards the dominant, C major. Here are intimations of birdsong (67) and a return to the main theme (69) in darker colours (four bassoons, half the violas, cellos). Violins provide a flowing counterpoint and the basses and other strings an on-beat pizzicato, while the quail calls above. It cannot last. The theme is not even complete when an abrupt crescendo intervenes (77). The earlier violin octaves (51–3, 57–8, subtly articulated as syncopations and crossing-over octave leaps) reappear, higher, in a more disturbed texture, and with intimations of minor modes in the woodwind, first D (79) then C (81–3).

With more of the dotted motif, again as if in 3/4, and a chromatic shift, the music emerges in seeming triumph onto B♭ with a big cadence (85–7). But this is the entry of the basses and the strangely alienated *idée fixe* (Ex. 6.3); the bass motif triumphs because the rising sequence of the *idée fixe* is never completed. In the first movement the sequence was extended as far as the high tonic C (see Ex. 4.3); here, rather than reaching high B♭, it is halted on A♭ (100), sustained while the bass motif, strengthened by violins, continues to rage.

This is the crisis: the music becomes more animated (100, 103) as the string motif gains in fury. A three-bar athematic crescendo brings a fortissimo, with two diminished sevenths (106–7) and the first entry of timpani – with wooden sticks, particularly harsh on the high F. All sense of tonal direction is lost and the metre is effectively suspended. The chords from 106 to 110 include the three possible diminished sevenths, with F minor and G minor at the ends of two bars (108–9). In the next bar every chord is off the beat (Ex. 6.5), the rhythm further confused by the *rallentando* before the harmony seems to settle. The last semiquaver of bar 110 is a C-major triad and the next bar suggests the dominant of F, which is both confirmed and challenged by the isolated low cello D♭ (112), potentially the upper neighbour to the cello's lowest note (the dominant), but not directly resolved.

When the wind enter above the D♭, in parallel thirds that recall the second statement of the main theme, the crisis appears to be over (Ex. 6.5, bar 113). At the elegant cadence, trills are another probably unconscious allusion to Beethoven's *Pastoral*.[12] Are rural tranquillity and hopefulness restored? The main theme returns in its original key (117), disguised as a stream of pizzicato semiquavers (the small notes in Ex. 6.5 show the derivation from the notes of the original theme; Berlioz's diminution required displacement of certain pitches relative to the beat).

Here a new melodic character appears on a solo clarinet (119), to which the flute adds respectful punctuation. This counter-theme includes the 'quail' rhythm derived from the original version of the main theme (121), and it echoes its own last phrase *pppp* (the word 'echo' appears in the score), but with D♭ rather than D♮, reversing the A♭–A♮ of the *idée fixe*.

When the clarinet adds its voice to the rising sequence (cf. 28–30), it grows impassioned and reaches a climactic e''' (sounding d'''), *sforzando* (130). This brings about a move to the dominant, unusual in a recapitulation. The main theme in its original note values (131) is played by second violins, so when seated correctly, on the right of the conductor, they are separated from the increasing bustle of the first violins. The counter-theme re-enters (133) with an additional whoop in its first bar but still *dolce*, and played by a wind quintet: flute, oboe, clarinet, horn, bassoon (the horn drops out for the echo). Like the previous C-major version of the main theme (from 69), this is incomplete. The bass remains on C throughout, increasingly sounding like a dominant pedal (from 139) that is duly resolved onto F at the top of the crescendo (143).

Example 6.5 'Scène aux champs', transition to reprise of the main theme

This *ff* chord (*f* in the wind) initiates the closing stages of the movement, a coda followed by the closing 'frame'. The *forte* quickly fades as the winds resume the cadential phrases of the main theme (cf. 44). The shape bracketed in Ex. 6.3 is passed to the strings for two bars of parallel triads; the tune is both top and bottom of the texture, something strictly forbidden according to a rule Berlioz probably enjoyed flouting; it sounds distinctive, its

83

Example 6.6 'Scène aux champs', combination of themes from bar 150

rise and fall perhaps reflecting the protagonist's breathing return-ing to normal. There follows a gentler cadence and, as in the previous movements, a reminiscence of the *idée fixe* (151). This time it is accommodated to the prevailing metre, and felicitously combined with two-bar fragments from the main theme, with the opening of the main theme in counterpoint with itself (Ex. 6.6).

The tied quavers return, but gently, and a passage in thirds and slow descending intervals introduces flats that might imply F minor; the last of these (bassoons, 158–9) becomes menacing, with lower strings (*tremolo*) and timpani re-entering after fifty bars of silence. Returning to a dominant (bass C), the next bars suggest more birdsong (flute, then clarinet); the opening of the *idée fixe* is again accommodated to the 6/8 metre, a calming effect soon challenged by a further crescendo and an upsurge of the cross-beat rhythm (164) which quickly fades; the hint of another crisis is averted, leaving soft gestures, perhaps of resignation, before the main part of the movement comes to rest (175).

The closing frame is longer than the opening. The cor anglais leaves space for the oboe to respond, but we hear only distant thunder. This, Hugh Macdonald has suggested, shows Berlioz not quite infallible in orchestration. He points out that 'there is no sense of F minor when three timpani roll the notes' of that chord, agreeing that 'Berlioz seems to have recognized this' when B♭ is added and the four timpani sound together.[13] But these are *sounds*, not intended to be heard as functional harmony: a touch of realism, reflecting the chaotic sound of thunder. The deployment of four timpani seems no less apposite than the four timpani in the March. The first three timpani entries, between cor anglais phrases, are all crescendo/diminuendo rolls, the third drum entering at or just before the loudest point. Sponge-headed sticks make pitches less distinct, so the first ostensible dissonance (A♭–B♭, 178) is not significant harmonically, and nor is the F-minor triad (183–5). After the four drums combine in the third entry, the intruder (B♭) is, logically enough, eliminated.

The cor anglais repeats its last phrase with more silences, slower and *perdendo*, a sigh of valediction. The herder's isolation echoes the protagonist's: 'Distant rumbling of thunder … solitude … silence'. Finally, strings in octaves slowly repeat the last three notes of the *ranz*, with a low horn (sounding C) hanging on, if the notation is literally observed, after the last string chords, a further symbol of isolation. Rural therapy has failed to cure the protagonist's malaise. The same instruments, timpani and horns, open the fourth movement in a very different spirit.

Notes

1. Raymond Monelle, *The Musical Topic. Hunt, Military and Pastoral* (Bloomington: Indiana University Press, 2006), 246.
2. Robert Schumann, 'A Symphony by Berlioz', in Bent (ed.), *Music Analysis in the Nineteenth Century* II, 167.
3. '… je souffrais affreusement, et je me couchai à terre, gémissant …, arrachant convulsivement des poignées d'herbe et d'innocentes pâquerettes …, luttant contre l'*absence*, contre l'horrible *isolement*'; *Mémoires* (ed. Bloom), 371.
4. Berlioz, 'De l'imitation musicale', in *Revue et Gazette Musicale* (1837). Berlioz, *Critique musicale* Vol. 3, 1–14; translation in Cone, *Fantastic Symphony*, 36–46.
5. 'Aperçu sur la musique et la musique romantique', *Le Correspondant* 1830). *Critique musicale* Vol. 1, 63–8; see also the foreword ('Avant-propos') to *Roméo et Juliette*, NBE Vol. 18, 2.
6. Raymond Monelle, *The Musical Topic*, 102.
7. Berlioz, *Berlioz on Music*, 92.
8. Berlioz, *Incomplete Operas* ed. Paul Banks and Ric Graebner (NBE Vol. 4) (Kassel: Bärenreiter, 2002), IX, which lists this chorus as one

of the later pieces, composed 1828–9. Grétry's *Guillaume Tell* (1791) adapts the call notated in Rousseau's *Dictionnaire de musique*; David Charlton, *Grétry and the Growth of Opéra-Comique* (Cambridge: Cambridge University Press, 1986), 313; Rousseau's entry reappears in *Encyclopédie méthodique (Musique)* (Paris: Chez Mme. veuve Agasse, 1818; reprint, New York: Da Capo Press, 1871), p. 97 of Supplément II.

9. Berlioz, *Grand traité*, ed. Bloom (NBE Vol. 24), 181; *Berlioz's Orchestration Treatise* (trans. Macdonald), 110.

10. My thanks to Frances Jones, author of a comprehensive study of alphorn music, for confirming this (personal communication).

11. Cited from Mark Evan Bonds, *The Beethoven Syndrome*, 187.

12. Beethoven, Sixth Symphony (*Pastoral*), second movement, bars 86, 112.

13. Hugh Macdonald, 'Berlioz's Orchestration: Human or Divine?' *The Musical Times* 110.1513 (March 1969): 255–8; cited 255.

FOURTH MOVEMENT

'Marche au supplice'

The 'Marche des gardes du franc-comte' was repackaged to form part of the autograph of *Symphonie fantastique*, with a fresh title-page pasted over the original.[1] Berlioz said that, whereas 'Scène aux champs' had taken a month of hard work, the March was written in a single night.[2] This need not mean finished to the last note; he followed the common compositional practice of writing the principal parts throughout to establish the form, filling in details later. The surviving libretto of *Les Francs-juges* suggests that the March may have been intended for Act II. Later, the hero, on the run from the tyrant and exhausted, experiences a flashback, and the main theme of the March is visible on the stubs of pages torn from the manuscript and destroyed. Although the March may have existed in some form in 1826, the autograph score is from 1829.[3]

The Opéra, where Berlioz first hoped this music would be heard, was equipped to stage crowd scenes and processions, normally grandiose rather than savage. Troops loyal to the tyrant in *Les Francs-juges*, intent on murder, were easily reconceived as guards marching to the place of execution. The ferocious first theme is set off by an exultant second theme, representing the hideous glee of the rabble hoping to witness an execution by guillotine (contemporary views, at least of the romantics, were not in favour of capital punishment).[4] But whatever Berlioz's programmatic intention, this movement is a symphonic 'portrait' of a march, unsuited to stage bands that usually employ only wind and percussion. The first distant sounds from a real band are bass drum thumps and piccolos rather than timpani and horns, and Berlioz's fierce main theme (*ff* when it enters) is not typical of his other marches. (To state that the opening conveys 'the sound of an approaching marching band' is to ignore the repeat: a band could not suddenly disappear and return.[5]) When he represented soldiers marching past in *Huit Scènes de Faust* (No. 7) he had done so realistically; distant fragments, a crescendo, coalescence of fragments into coherent phrases, then fragmentation in diminuendo.

The movement's form is relatively simple. The only alteration needed to fit the programme was a memory of the *idée fixe* tacked onto the end, the dreamer's last vision of the beloved before the guillotine falls. In Table 7.1, 'X' represents a transitional passage. The march begins, fortuitously given its origins, with the instruments that close 'Scène aux champs' – timpani and horns – but with a difference; instead of distant rumbling, the timpani beat a tattoo (though with sponge-headed sticks), and the horns have a marked rhythm (♩♩♩) that reappears in theme 2. Berlioz required the timpanists to use two sticks on the first and third beats of each bar, the other notes to be played with the right hand only rather than, as would seem natural, left and right in alternation. This should check any tendency to take the March, as Norman del Mar says, 'at a spanking pace which cuts directly against its gruesome and menacing character'; faster than Berlioz's ♩ = 72, 'the remarkable technique which Berlioz requires of the timpanists becomes frankly impossible'.[6]

The horns use pitches outside the natural harmonic series, requiring hand-stopping. Even if equipped with valves, they should mix open and stopped notes, and any resulting inconsistency of timbre adds to the movement's character. The clarinets, formerly in B♭ and A, are now in C, not the obvious choice for a movement in G minor where the second theme, each time it

Table 7.1 *Form of 'Marche au supplice'*

1	18	62–77	78	114	164–78
Introduction	Theme 1, reiterated	Theme 2 (wind band)	X; repeat of theme 2; X	Theme 1	Coda: *idée fixe* cut short; uproar
G minor	g–E♭-g	B♭	g–B♭–g	g–D♭	G–g–G

7 Fourth Movement 'Marche au supplice'

Example 7.1 'Marche au supplice', main theme

comes, is in the relative major, B♭. It is now standard practice to play C clarinet parts on the B♭ instrument, transposing at sight, but here and in the finale Berlioz chose smaller clarinets, not for convenience but for their brighter (or harsher) tone quality. The lower brass appear for the first time in the symphony: three tenor trombones and two ophicleides, for which tubas are substituted in modern-instrument performance. Five percussionists may be needed, with three on timpani at the end; cymbals and bass drum on the final chord can be hit by one player, with another on side drum. Berlioz's deployment of these instruments is considerably more subtle than the regular accentuation of the main beats typical in functional marches and, if Berlioz is to be believed, in certain operas; the excessive zeal of the bass-drum player forms a thread in the linking matter between stories in *Les Soirées de l'orchestre*.

The sixteen-bar introduction is a dialogue between the timpani tattoo and the horn responses, amplified by woodwind and low brass. An abrupt crescendo to a *tutti* chord (bar 17) launches the main theme (Ex. 7.1).

First heard on its own, the eight-bar theme is reiterated four times: first with a counterpoint in the bassoons' tenor register (24); then twice in E♭ (33, 41); then back in G minor (49) with a stream of bassoon quavers (Ex. 7.2). Four bassoons were normal in French orchestras; traditional French instruments, rather than the German type prevailing in modern orchestras, enhance the grotesque character of these counterpoints. Their slightly buzzing attack may be heard on older French recordings and from period-instrument orchestras.

Example 7.2 'Marche au supplice', main theme, with inversion and counterpoint

After two low-register statements, the third and fourth are on violins, with a new counterpoint (cellos and basses) combined with the timpani tattoo from the introduction. All statements begin loudly, followed by a diminuendo, until the last (49) which is *piano*, pizzicato, and with the theme in the bass mirrored by its inversion on upper strings. The bassoons, mostly in unison but sometimes in octaves or thirds, range over three octaves from their tenor register to their bottom note (Ex. 7.2).

In a nod to the regularity normally required for marching, up to this point Berlioz has untypically presented no fewer than seven successive eight-bar units. The last is extended by an additional five bars as the theme fragments; the bassoons continue their counterpoint, and a sweeping scale (61) jolts the music to B♭ major. The second theme (Ex. 7.3) is a pair of matching eight-bar phrases woven of deliberately coarse fabric, and initiated by the horn rhythm of the introduction: typical march material. The bass at the cadence into the theme is played by the third (tenor) trombone, landing on the low B♭ recently vacated by the bassoons. Only tenor trombones in B♭ were generally available in Paris; Berlioz laments the absence of alto and bass instruments in an article of 1837.[7] The low B♭ is a 'pedal-note', the instrument's fundamental with the slide retracted. In his Requiem ('Hostias') Berlioz asks the players to descend lower, to F♯, by means of the slide. Pedal notes were not in common use, and Berlioz says their existence was unknown to many trombonists.[8] He describes their tone as noble rather than coarse, and in 'Marche au supplice' he marks them *mezzo-forte* against the *forte* of the rest of the band. Here horns can use their 'cylindres', though if hand-stopping were used in the general melee, with high woodwind, cornets, and trumpets also playing, any unevenness of horn tone would pass unnoticed.

The sixteen-bar theme is two eight-bar phrases in 'antecedent–consequent' succession, with bars 9–12 the same as 1–4; Ex. 7.3 shows the antecedent. The theme comes three times if the formal repeat is observed, the third (89) being shortly after the repeat. But overall, this section is not regular in phrase lengths; after the double bar, before the third statement, are eleven bars (X in Table 7.1) that toss a figure between brass and woodwind, followed by fragments of the main theme (pizzicato) punctuated by an orchestral novelty: the last beat of bar 84 is played by percussion only. The second theme (89) is texturally filled out by strings and introduced by four timpani producing an arpeggio in the rhythm of the introduction.

Berlioz had no need to alter the March's character when he transferred it to the symphony; its later stages were already

Example 7.3 'Marche au supplice', second theme

nightmarish. After theme 2, the X material (105; cf. 78) recurs, covering nine bars. The first theme (114) recovers its original note values, on low brass and bassoons in parallel triads, with a harsh string accompaniment (*ff* against the other instruments' *mf*). A massive *ff* version follows after nine bars, further eroding its earlier regularity while restoring the theme's original diminuendos.

There follows what some have considered nothing less than a harmonic outrage: the last bar of the theme that set out in G minor (123) lands instead on a chord of Db (130). The theme is restated in inversion in that key, the furthest removed from G minor in the tonal spectrum. Both iterations are on wind and low strings, accompanied by screaming upper-string tremolo. The Db version explodes into fragments after only five bars, lurching back to G minor and setting up a reiteration of a dotted rhythm related to the second theme (140). G-minor cadences suggest that we are approaching or already in a coda, but after twelve bars the strings plunge down over nearly two octaves, mainly on a scale of G minor. Woodwind pick up the dotted rhythm (154, with a silent first beat), quite offensively from the point of view of traditional harmony, since they play a chord of D♭. The passage dies down with G minor and D♭ alternating on wind and strings until the wind yield, changing a few notes in a diminuendo to near silence; explosive dominant chords (160) prepare for closure.

The movement must originally have ended at bar 164. The return to the dominant at the half-bar is immediately followed by the *idée fixe*, rudely cut off before completing its first phrase. In a further alternation, now of mode, G minor (164) is followed by the first phrase of the *idée fixe* (unaccompanied) in G major. The guillotine and falling head (pizzicato) are in G minor, with the last nine bars a ghoulishly gleeful G major.

Even without this programmatic ending, 'Marche au supplice' is a remarkable exercise in stretching expectations, harmonic, instrumental, and formal, both suggesting and defying the 'March topic'. This is not originality for its own sake, but aims at a Breughel-esque image of a ritual action accompanied by an unruly crowd. The modernism that repelled some of Berlioz's contemporaries perhaps reaches back unconsciously to the past; tales of the French revolutionary terror may have been the prime inspiration for this nightmare vision, its music – like that of much of the finale – both coarse and subtle.

Notes

1. Facsimiles of both title pages: NBE 16, 183–4.
2. *Memoirs*, chap. 26; *Mémoires* (ed. Bloom), 274; *The Memoirs* (trans. Cairns), 104.
3. Holoman, *The Creative Process*, 224–7.
4. Bloom, 'Berlioz in the Year of the *Symphonie fantastique*', 3.
5. Julia Kursell, 'Hearing in the Music of Hector Berlioz', in David Trippett and Benjamin Walton (eds.), *Nineteenth-Century Opera and the Scientific Imagination* (Cambridge: Cambridge University Press, 2019), 109–33; cited 117.
6. Norman del Mar, *Conducting Berlioz*, 31.
7. Berlioz, 'Strauss, son orchestra, ses valses. – De l'avenir du rhythme'. Trans. Julian Rushton, 'Johann Strauss and the Future of Rhythm', *Berlioz Society Bulletin* 212 (January 2021), 43–53.
8. Berlioz, *Grand Traité*, ed. Bloom (NBE Vol. 24), 303; Macdonald, *Berlioz's Orchestration Treatise*, 214.

8

FIFTH MOVEMENT

'Songe d'une nuit de Sabbat'

The finale is a composite movement, but its subdivision into slow and fast tempi is not at all like that between the first movement's Largo and Allegro. Only the first twenty bars are slow. The Allegro tempo is maintained for the rest of the movement with variations in the exact speed, metronomically indicated. The Allegro is started by the grotesque transformation (signalled in the programme) of the *idée fixe* into a jig. There follows a kind of funeral ritual for the dreaming protagonist that introduces and burlesques the *Dies irae* plainchant, still notated in the fast 6/8, although much of this section sounds slower because of the chant's long note values. The main subdivision within the Allegro is after 240 bars out of 524, so nearly halfway in bar length, and indeed in duration; it is headed 'Ronde du Sabbat'. This starts ironically as an academically correct fugue and climaxes when the fugue subject is combined with the *Dies irae*. Numerous orchestral innovations provided a model for the musically grotesque and 'fantastique' in later works by Berlioz and others. A detailed table would be over-complicated; Table 8.1 presents a simple outline.

Anything claimed as unprecedented may seem so only because precedents have not been identified, but Berlioz's finale is certainly a piece for which such a claim might reasonably be made. Early reception (especially rejection) suggests that it seemed, at least, novel. It perplexed the generally sympathetic Schumann, and disgusted Mendelssohn when he looked at the score in Rome.[1] Students to whom I showed the opening pages without identifying the composer assumed it was music from the early twentieth century. A better guess might have been Liszt; the third movement ('Mephistopheles') of his *Faust* symphony begins with a similar bass figure. If one did not know that the composers were still on good terms, one might suspect that Liszt's *ironico* implied a parody of Berlioz (Ex. 8.1).

Table 8.1 *Formal outline of 'Songe d'une nuit de Sabbat'*

Larghetto $\downarrow = 63$	21 Allegro $\downarrow . = 112^{(a)}$	102	241 $\downarrow . = 104$	414
Introduction	*Idée fixe* and welcome	Ritual: *Dies irae*; transition (222)	'Ronde du Sabbat'	Union of themes; coda (496)
Indeterminate in key	C–E♭	C Dorian	C, fugal exposition	C/A minor/C

(a) At bar 29, Allegro assai $\mathbf{O} = 76$; at bar 40, Allegro $\downarrow . = 104$, which is repeated at bar 241 where Berlioz notes: 'The tempo, which should have quickened a little, returns here to that of bar 40' ('Le mouvement, qui a dû s'animer un peu, redevient ici, comme à la 40me mesure, $\downarrow . = 104$').

Example 8.1 (a) Berlioz, 'Songe d'une nuit de Sabbat'; (b) Liszt, 'Mephistopheles' (*Eine Faust-Sinfonie*)

There are obvious differences: the tempo, the high *tremolo* in Berlioz, the high wind and pizzicato chord in Liszt. The attack following the bass motif includes a timpani chord in Berlioz and unpitched percussion (triangle, cymbal) in Liszt. However, both chords are diminished sevenths, and both bass figures cover the same interval, the tritone (diminished fifth), an interval with diabolic associations appropriate to the dramatic context of each symphony.

Example 8.2 'Songe d'une nuit de Sabbat', bars 11–12

Returning to Berlioz's opening: the high G that ended the March recurs, but *pianissimo*, part of the tonally indeterminate diminished seventh chord (A♯–C♯–E–G) that lasts about twelve seconds. Other pitches appear as passing notes when the woodwind (bassoons divided into four) take over the chord. There are precedents for starting a movement on a dissonance; Beethoven's String Quartet Op. 59 No. 3 starts on a diminished seventh. By now Berlioz had probably read with some puzzlement the acute dissonance that opens the finale of Beethoven's Ninth Symphony.[2] Yet this can be understood functionally in relation to the main key, whereas Berlioz's chord simply dissolves into a chromatic slide that could have landed anywhere. That it arrives on the symphony's tonic, C major, is a happy accident, but a solid tonal centre cannot be established so arbitrarily, and growling basses hint at C minor with their A flats.

A second diminished seventh (F♯–A–C–E♭) also lasts about twelve seconds (6–9), with a touch of sulphur from the trombones; while it is sustained, piccolo, flute, and oboe offer a new rhythm and an octave glissando, echoed by a horn – eerie, like Mahler's 'cry of nature' (*Naturlaut*) in his Third Symphony (fourth movement). How the glissando is to be produced is not explained; Berlioz may have intended the woodwind players to cover the holes in rapid succession, and/or relax the embouchure (either would sound more eerie than the fast chromatic scale one sometimes hears). A still weirder invention is bar 11, an arpeggio passed from lower to higher instruments and consisting mainly of fourths, perfect and augmented, with three minor thirds (Ex. 8.2) – not the arpeggio of perfect fourths that inaugurates Schönberg's first Chamber Symphony (1906), but scarcely less radical. This lands on the third of the three possible diminished sevenths (B–D–F–A♭).

This nightmarish introduction is deliberately unformed in harmony, sonority, and motivic shapes; bars 5 and 11 are passing incidents, never repeated. The arrival of the third diminished seventh hints at order, repeating bars 1–4 a semitone higher; had this continued it would have landed on D♭ but instead it settles on A♭ (16), established by the growling basses (although pitches at that register are difficult to distinguish). The next bar adds F♯ to form the augmented sixth that usually functions as preparation for the dominant; conveniently, it includes the note C, allowing the *Naturlaut* to be repeated.

These twenty fragmentary bars offer nothing suited to extension and development. What follows is another kind of disorder, but the changes of metre and tempo are clarified by the programme: when Allegro is twice indicated with 6/8 time signature (21, 40), the clarinet in C and the small clarinet in E♭ in turn play the *idée fixe* as a vulgar jig. Curiously, the full statement of the *idée fixe* from bar 40 should be a little slower than bar 21. The C clarinet is *ppp* and marked *lointain* (distant), although no time is allowed for the player to leave the stage and return, and it participates in the welcoming uproar (*Allegro assai*, 29, in 2/2) that obliterates the key of C in eleven athematic bars. In the protagonist's nightmare, *she* is coming. When she arrives and seems to dance, the E♭ clarinet, warmed up by joining the *tutti*, plays the entire *idée fixe* with a coarse accompaniment and simple harmonization. The piccolo joins in as the texture thickens.

The Ritual

This version of the *idée fixe* establishes the tempo and metre for the rest of the movement apart from a 2/2 bar (81) at the same speed, accommodating four equal crotchets (as in the Scherzo of Beethoven's *Eroica* symphony, where equal minims abruptly fill bars of 3/4). However, the principal tonality of the movement, and the whole symphony, is yet to be established.

Much of the passage that follows the *idée fixe* cadence (64) sounds slower because of the long gaps between each bell chime, and the initial solemnity of the plainchant in whole-bar notes (Ex. 8.3). The overall harmonic trajectory is towards C major,

Example 8.3 'Songe d'une nuit de Sabbat', bells and *Dies irae*

but before the *Dies irae* the key of E♭ is undermined by tending, in the final stages of the uproar, towards C minor. The *Dies irae* itself is in the Dorian mode on C, starting on the (minor) mediant; the first phrase ends when C is preceded by a flattened seventh, B♭ (the seven-note mode is completed by the A that appears in the second phrase). The bells at bar 121, their C clashing with the strings' C♯, are a delayed echo of their first two entries (102, 110); they return *forte* on the last note of the first phrase of the plainchant.

Tonally, there is double transition from E♭ to C major, the latter only fully confirmed at the heading 'Ronde du Sabbat' (241). The first step in this double transition is the C-minor uproar (from 65) that overwhelms the *idée fixe* cadence and shifts to A♭ and back (69–70). There is more disorder in the chromatic scales (72–5), despite an emphatic dominant of C (76–7), broken by descending athematic thirds; the 'dreadful band of ghosts, sorcerers, and all kinds of monsters' seems to be reverting to chaos. But unlike the curious arpeggios of thirds in the first-movement exposition (bars 115–33), or the finale's own weird arpeggio (Ex. 8.2), this descent ends solidly on a dominant of C minor (82).

The major-minor uncertainty is expressed by a pitch conflict between the mediants, E♭ and E♮. The short thematic fragment (84–5) that later starts the fugue subject (241) here adds to the uncertainty by ending in mid-air on E♮ (85), instantly contradicted by the lower instruments' E♭ and another descent, at first by thirds, that turns into a slow scale down to bottom C. The fugue-subject fragment is reiterated by violas in C minor (107), then disappears for over 100 bars.

The section with bells and the *Dies irae* can be understood as a kind of black requiem, the dreamer witnessing his own funeral. Low bells (or pianos) are given long note values and the chime is always C, C, G. If pianos are used (in double octaves with middle C (c') the highest pitch), Berlioz wrote 'Grande pédale', probably intending the sustaining pedal to be held down throughout the section; similarly the bell chimes should not be damped but allowed to die away (though the usual instruction 'laissez vibrer' – 'let ring' – is not in the score). The bell entries are not, as one might expect, evenly spaced; the first three are separated by eight, then eleven bars.[3]

The violas and a few other orchestral gestures remind the listener of the 6/8 momentum that soon comes fully into play. Each phrase of the *Dies irae* is first heard as it might be in church: on low instruments, four bassoons and two ophicleides (one standing in for the serpent). The first two phrases, of eight and twelve bars, are punctuated by the bells that seem to enter prematurely (see Ex. 8.3). This is the first hint that the solemnity of the chant is to be undermined by outright parody. Trombones play each phrase at double speed, in coarse parallel triads; fiendish mockery is still more obvious when the high woodwind and pizzicato strings turn the grave chant into a jig.

The chant ends in a flicker of brilliance (221), and the second transition unfolds over a bass drum roll (using timpani sticks). Fragments of the upcoming fugue subject reappear: in G, in E♭, and then most strikingly in E minor (230), the previous pitch conflict becoming a clash of keys; E minor is the pivot that eliminates C minor and establishes C major for the remainder of the movement. After eight bars of E minor, its relative G, the home dominant, asserts itself for the grand cadence into bar 241, and the jaunty fugue begins.

'Ronde du Sabbat'

I have called the burlesque of the *idée fixe* a jig, but the savage joy of the Round Dance may be what tempts conductors to adopt a tempo more suited to a tarantella, an Italian dance cultivated by several composers including Berlioz's friends Stephen Heller and Camille Saint-Saëns, or saltarello, as in the finale of Mendelssohn's 'Italian' symphony. However, the tempo is only ♩. = 104 whereas Berlioz's own saltarello, in his overture *Le Carnaval romain*, is ♩. = 156. As the fugue begins (241), Berlioz cautions the conductor to rein in the tempo a little ('Un peu retenu') following the *animez un peu* (223). Perhaps the long crescendo to the climactic combination of the *Dies irae* and the fugue subject (414) may suggest an *accelerando*, but it is undesirable to exceed Berlioz's original tempo by much, if at all, until the coda, where he again writes *animez un peu*: a little faster, not a lot.

The fugue, though unorthodox in details, restores a degree of order that even the most austere professor should not overlook. Schumann noted that the first entries are academically correct, unlike a number of Berlioz's later fugal expositions, notably the magnificent 'Judex crederis' in his *Te Deum*. Table 8.2 summarizes how Berlioz both retained and broke down his fugal material, with episodes and variations prior to the combination with the *Dies irae* at bar 414.

The exposition is in four 'voices' (strings). Another orthodox fugal practice, as well as the correct answer at the fifth, is that Berlioz provided two regular countersubjects, as he took care to do in his Rome Prize fugues, in accordance with the rules. Decidedly not academically prim is the rough punctuation from brass and bassoons (Ex. 8.4). While here it is apparently a gesture of contempt at academe, similar punctuation is used, surely with no satirical intention, in the fugal 'Libera me' of Verdi's Requiem.

The first twenty-bar episode (269) starts as vigorous counterpoint with an apparent intention to modulate by sequence, as fugal episodes often do. But this is a 'Ronde du Sabbat', not a sacred work, and this intention is abandoned after only eight bars. The rest of the episode consists of an athematic upsurge and unison bars based entirely on semitones; these could be loosely related to

Table 8.2 'Ronde du Sabbat' considered as a fugue

241	269	289	305	331	347	364	386
Exposition (four parts)	Episode	Middle entries	Episode	Variations	Episode *Dies irae*	Subject entries (4)	Stretto
C–G–C–G		G–C		Key fluctuates	G minor?	G–C	C

Example 8.4 'Ronde du Sabbat', fugue subject, countersubjects, and punctuation

the neighbour-note figure in the Florian song and the *idée fixe*. Typical of Berlioz's vision of this 'dreadful band of ghosts, sorcerers, and all kinds of monsters' are the dynamic changes and giddy shifts of tonal orientation, for example, the emphatic, even triumphant, E♭–A♭ (286–7); but this is promptly negated by a jump to the dominant of G.

The next two fugal entries restore some decorum, although these 'middle entries' begin in G minor for two bars, before being 'corrected' by the bass entry in G major (291), dutifully answered in C (298). Both countersubjects are revived, as is the brass punctuation, but the texture is fuller. The second subject-entry ends, effectively preventing any third entry, by an ascending diatonic scale that adds flats as it goes along, reaching E♭ (305). This the brass instruments gleefully confirm, as they do the next solid chords, at five-bar intervals. Each is approached by sixfold flickering figures, semitones in the wind, three-note motifs in the strings, exchanged across orchestral sections. Remarkably, the first notes of the violin motif outline a descending whole-tone scale: D–C–B♭–G♯–F♯–E, completed by the lower D within the brass chord (310). This process is repeated up a tone, except that the final F♯ is deferred for two bars, the brass chord sticking to A♭. The woodwinds' third gasping chromatic descent, still mainly using 6–3 (first inversion) triads, is counterpointed by violins, pizzicato, ascending in triads rooted a whole tone apart (F♯–E–D–C–B♭–A♭).

This was not Berlioz's first use of a whole-tone scale, but it is more audible here than in bars 620–3 of the *Francs-juges* overture. In the symphony, the strings start by picking up the last note of each semitone gasp (as 306–7: flute E♭–D, violins starting on D an octave lower). The third version of this idea, with pizzicato chords, has the wind picking up the roots of the violin chords. I discuss this remarkable passage at some length, because it shows Berlioz fortuitously ahead of his time even if he did not quite realize what he had done; there is nothing comparable to the brazen whole-tone scale in Glinka's overture *Ruslan and Lyudmila*, composed only a few years later.

No doubt for programmatic reasons, Berlioz adds effect after effect, something that, given the legacy his orchestral imagination offered to later composers, has too often been held against him. The brass D♭ (unison, 320) initiates a kind of panic. The high woodwind and pizzicato violins interlock to form a chromatic descent, a kind of 'hocket', although Berlioz probably knew nothing of this mediaeval procedure.

This second episode recovers something like normality from bar 327 with string motifs and a horn fanfare, although these, too, are isolated incidents rather than contributions to motivic coherence. The horns are in different keys (I in E♭, III in C), notated a minor third apart but sounding in unison, with a few stopped notes, including the final accented E♭ of the third horn. In his treatise Berlioz classified the tone quality of this as 'good', but if modern chromatic horns play it 'open' a nuance of timbre is lost, and with an accent it could legitimately be 'cuivré', the almost percussive (or sneezing) attack sometimes represented (as in Wagner's scores) by + above the note. The same stopped note is used in the introduction to Act II of Beethoven's *Fidelio*, depicting the unlit dungeon. Berlioz used 'sons bouchés', including one note he had described in the treatise as 'bad', for the demonic 'evocation' in *La Damnation de Faust*.[4] A few bars on (370, 372) chromatic horns, if available, are told to play the normally open C stopped ('bouchés avec les cylindres'), and the *sforzando* could produce the 'cuivré' effect.

The next episode, were this movement aspiring to be read as a sonata form, would be considered 'development' because of the idiosyncratic variation, or distortion, of the fugue subject. Rather than moving by steps, it is turned into rising and falling arpeggios while keeping its original rhythm (331). This idea is exchanged between lower strings and bassoons, with rapid harmonic changes undermining any residual tonal stability. G minor is reached (347), but as if in the Dorian mode, with ghostly reminiscences of the *Dies irae* on cellos and horns, the latter marked 'solo' and requiring several stopped notes.

Violas propose another distortion of the fugue subject (355), its shape now compressed by using nothing but semitones. This is taken up after another *Dies irae* fragment, and over a bass-drum roll this chromatic subject is treated to a four-part counter-exposition (from 364), necessarily without the original counter-subjects. The later entries follow at lengthening intervals after four, five, six, and seven bars, the last entry (379) falling into sequential repetitions of a two-bar unit. The whole section is marked 'crescendo' and reaches a *tutti* diminished seventh, syncopated so that for eight bars the metre sounds like 3/4; when the

Example 8.5 'Ronde du Sabbat' and *Dies irae* combined

brass enter (399) two 3/4 metres clash with each other until 6/8 is restored (403), with the E♭–E♮ referring back to the earlier transition into the 'Ronde'.

After a few false starts (from 404) comes a clear reprise (407), the fugue subject exultantly on strings in unison. The answer in the dominant (414) acquires a new countersubject: nothing less than the *Dies irae*. In the score Berlioz proudly headed this moment 'Dies irae et Ronde du Sabbat ensemble', also the last words of the programme (Ex. 8.5). It might be thought that he anticipated twentieth-century bitonality at this point, as the subject/answer sets off in G while the *Dies irae*, since it starts on C, is in a modal A minor. It hardly sounds bitonal, however, and the fugue subject soon dissolves into passagework; the complete subject only fits against the plainchant for six bars. The basses seem to try restoring the tonic C via its dominant, preceded as in the first movement by an A♭ (426), but the plainchant dominates, ending firmly on A♮. The other instruments are compelled to accept this (435), and A minor is maintained as a local tonic for some twenty bars.

This relative minor (A) is extended over five bars with growling basses (435), then by units of four bars: the first four, violent hockets on dominant harmony and the next four, still athematic, a clattering on high strings played percussively. Berlioz writes 'frappez avec le bois de l'archet': strike with the wood of the bow (*col legno*). Each section's rhythm is carefully arranged to disagree with the others. The fugue subject enters in A minor on the first cellos (upbeat to 448), but not as we have heard it before: it is augmented rhythmically and decorated with trills. Meanwhile the clatter continues above, and the texture is completed by the pizzicato counterpoint on second cellos and basses. The *col legno* was not a common direction at this time, nor was the division of the cello section. The *col legno* is more percussive than definite in pitch, and even Liszt's skill in transcribing could not replicate the effect; instead, he added a gratuitous word, 'burlesque', to the cello entry.

A fugal answer in D minor seems to be proposed (upbeat to 460), but it is aborted. Instead the woodwind have an extraordinary passage of athematic chatter, like a flock of angry jays. It is not as chaotic as it sounds, being internally ordered by sequences in four-part harmony (460–6). Even such magical evocations as *Danse macabre* by Saint-Saëns and *L'Apprenti sorcier* by Paul Dukas (a Berlioz admirer) lose some claim to originality from this short episode.

The woodwind chatter lands on E minor (467) for a furious *tutti*. The nightmarish sequence of events continues with violent dynamic contrasts and a merry gallop to an explosive diminished seventh on the half-bar (484). There seems by this time no need to resolve such a chord with any degree of linear orthodoxy, although if it were respelled as E–G–B♭–D♭ (rather than C♯) it could be considered as a dominant of the next harmony, which is F minor (485). The following bars – half *pp* and half *ff* with a rolled bass drum added to string tremolo – bring a last reminiscence of the *Dies irae*. Its first five notes (bassoons, ophicleides) are rudely repeated, as before, by trombones at double speed and a fifth higher, duly followed by the jig-like woodwind version.

A massive cadence allows us to identify bar 496 as the beginning of the coda. There is a last but clear reminiscence of the *idée fixe*; it reappears as if blended with the fugue subject, identifiable by the melodic succession bracketed in Ex. 8.6, and the sequence up to B♭.

Like other Berlioz codas, this emphasizes its closing function by repeated cadences interrupted by alien triads, as here; the sequence derived from the *idée fixe* reaches A but leaps arbitrarily (I use the word without pejorative intent) by a tritone to a chord of E♭ (508), quickly unravelled for a further V–I cadence. That settles

Example 8.6 'Songe d'une nuit de Sabbat', final allusion to the *idée fixe*

the issue, bar some chromatic sulphur from trombones (at least, it is trombones that one mostly hears), with more cadences and a five-bar C major *tutti*. The last chord is to be held ('tenu'), with a cymbal to be struck by a sponge-headed stick; all too often licentious percussionists, perhaps at the conductor's suggestion, clash a pair of cymbals and hold them up in triumph.

***

What are we to make of all this? If the first movement was a stream of consciousness, as Elliott Carter suggested, this finale is the more random – because semi-conscious – stream of a nightmare. This point was not appreciated by Berlioz's earliest critic, François-Joseph Fétis, and even Schumann in his response to Fétis gave up before the end (see Chapter 10). Another who did not appreciate it, admittedly (as with Schumann) without yet having heard it, was Mendelssohn; writing home from Rome in 1831, he was distressed to see Berlioz, 'that friendly, quiet and meditative person', so confident of his 'contrived passion, represented by every possible exaggerated orchestral means [he gives accurate details of some of these] to express nothing but indifferent drivel, mere grunting, shouting, screaming back and forth'.[5] Mendelssohn's language is strikingly reminiscent of the reactions of his own teacher in Berlin, Carl Friedrich Zelter, who examined the printed score of *Huit Scènes de Faust* that Berlioz had sent to Goethe in homage to the poet, and at his request; Zelter reported that the composer was one of those people who could only attract attention by 'coughs, snorts, croaks and spitting'.[6]

Chaos was nothing new in music, recent manifestations being by Haydn (the opening of *The Creation*) and Beethoven, where the harshest dissonance (all seven notes of the 'harmonic' minor

scale) is banished in the final movement of his Ninth Symphony
when the voice enters with 'Oh friends, not these sounds, but let us
hear something more agreeable' (words by Beethoven himself to
precede the setting of Schiller's *Ode to Joy*). Earlier attempts to
convey chaos in music were probably unknown to Berlioz, but he
alluded to *The Creation* in his essay on musical imitation, which
starts as a review of Giuseppe Carpani's book on Haydn and is
mostly concerned with Haydn's imitations of nature.[7]

Berlioz's, or his protagonist's, nightmare ends in a blaze of
C major, but it is not the triumph of joy, friendship, or freedom
of Beethoven's Fifth and Ninth Symphonies (respectively in C and
D major), or the C-major blaze of light that follows the 'represen-
tation of chaos' in *The Creation*. Rather it is the glaring light that
wakens Berlioz's *alter ego* from his deep sleep, confused, surprised to be alive, and soon to be consoled by other kinds of music
in the sequel *Lélio, ou Le Retour à la vie*, discussed in the next
chapter.

Notes

1. R. Larry Todd, *Mendelssohn: A Life in Music* (New York: Oxford
   University Press, 2003), 238–9.
2. Berlioz, *À travers chants*, 57–8; (ed. Léon Guichard), 75.
3. On the spacing of the bell chimes, see Rushton, *The Music of
   Berlioz*, 255.
4. Berlioz, *Grand Traité* (ed. Bloom, NBE Vol. 24), 273; Macdonald,
   Berlioz's Orchestration Treatise (trans. Macdonald), 166–72.
5. Translation in Cone, *Fantastic Symphony*, 281–2; cited, 282.
6. *Briefwechsel zwischen Goethe und Zelter in den Jahren 1796 bis 1832*
   (Berlin, 1833–4), letter 662.
7. Translation in Cone, *Fantastic Symphony*, 36–46.

THE SEQUEL

Reception by Composers

Berlioz's name is inextricably associated with *Symphonie fantastique*, which is sometimes seen as almost his only work to be counted as important, at least in the sense of 'historically significant'. That importance derives from its musical originality. Even disregarding the programme, its formal freedoms, its having one theme appear in each movement, its theatrical use of off-stage instruments, and Berlioz's resourceful and imaginative orchestral writing justify the twenty-odd pages in Richard Taruskin's monumental history of Western music.[1] Taruskin does not disregard the programme, and heads his discussion 'Instrumental Drama'; but he has little to say about Berlioz's other works.

The programme itself was not much imitated, at least in its wealth of detail, and was often deplored. Another departure from conventional decorum was Berlioz's evocation of the grotesque, which led to some good musicians having difficulties in appreciating it. Earlier composers had varied musical shapes by speeding them up or presenting them in comical or violent ways, but such procedures were not usually applied to a long melody or a sacred chant. It seems Berlioz was not afraid to give offence, and he could not have been surprised by some of the adverse responses to his work.

Lélio, ou le Retour à la Vie

The first creative response to *Symphonie fantastique* was its sequel, the *mélologue Lélio*, originally called *Le Retour à la vie*. This responds to the symphony's programme rather than to the music. The audience on 9 December 1832 heard both works together: this bold step of unifying a concert programme was one that the composer returned to with *Roméo et Juliette* and *La*

Damnation de Faust. Yet when the works were repeated on 30 December the concert included other pieces, as if the complete 'Episode in an artist's life' were not enough of a temptation to buy tickets. The combination *Symphonie fantastique–Lélio* was revived in Weimar on 21 February 1855, conducted by Berlioz, with Liszt, who masterminded Berlioz's visits to the city, himself participating.[2]

Lélio is written for tenor and baritone soloists, chorus, and an accomplished actor who represents the symphony's protagonist; he speaks, sighs, and emotes, but does not sing. He is 'Lélio', a name close to 'Berlioz' if the latter's final Z is not pronounced (as it usually is). No doubt Berlioz hoped that the two works together would become a standard concert item. A note added in 1855 reads:

the programme should be distributed to the audience whenever the symphony is performed *dramatically* and followed by its sequel, the monodrama Lélio, which completes the *episode in the life of an artist*. In this case, the invisible orchestra is seated on the stage of the theatre, behind a lowered curtain.[3]

These two works of disparate genre were never published together, and the symphony is nearly always heard on its own. In 1855 a full score of *Lélio* appeared, together with a vocal score prepared by a young and expert pianist, none other than Camille Saint-Saëns. The monologues are interspersed with six pieces not originally composed for this context, but the protagonist refers to them as either his own earlier compositions or as music he imagines and might, perhaps, later compose. In the final version the speaker both begins and ends the *mélologue*, and this version forms the basis of the following discussion.

The symphony itself, if it precedes *Lélio*, should be performed invisibly, with the actor, front of stage, pretending to sleep. He wakes having expected to die: 'God!' he exclaims, 'I'm alive ... What a dreadful night'. His suicide note is in his hand; he recalls his friend 'Horatio' (not the last allusion to *Hamlet*) singing his favourite *mélodie – Le Pêcheur*, a song for high tenor and piano derived from Goethe's ballad of a fisherman lured to a watery grave by a siren. 'Lélio' says he had written this song a few years earlier, but this does not determine the song's actual date; a letter from Rome to the translator (Berlioz's friend Albert du Boys) implies that he had only recently received the poem and appropriated ('emparé') his setting for 'this strange work' ('cette singulière composition'), the mélologue.[4] So Lélio's dating is poetic licence. The song was later published on its own. In the mélologue, it is paused while hidden violins play the *idée fixe*, unaccompanied; the actor utters the word 'Sirène'.

This links the song to the symphony and Berlioz's own suffering in love, but it is unfair to Harriet Smithson, who was certainly no siren. Rather than luring Berlioz to her, she refused to meet him until after the 1832 premiere of *Lélio*. The slur on her character derives from rumours put about in 1830 by Berlioz's fiancée Camille Moke that Smithson was unchaste (she was not). In the eyes of Berlioz's family, any female associated with the theatre was likely to be unchaste, and here in the *mélologue* one might be tempted to infer a touch of misogyny. On the whole, however, Berlioz should escape this charge. The many women in his life were friends as well as family and lovers; his sisters were close confidantes, and he supported the efforts of the composer Louise Bertin in staging *Esmeralda*. He created several leading roles for dramatic mezzo-sopranos (the voice type of his second wife, Marie Recio), all well characterized and attracting audience sympathy both in joy and suffering. In *La Damnation de Faust*, Berlioz follows his model, Goethe, by ending with Marguerite's salvation. He was in love with the heroines Cassandra and Dido (*Les Troyens*), and in his last opera *Béatrice et Bénédict* his departures from Shakespeare's *Much Ado about Nothing* include the enhancement of both female roles. Beatrice, after a grand scena of a type no male character is allowed in this opera, remains fully Benedict's equal in the closing duet, whereas in Shakespeare she is silenced with a kiss, leaving the last words to the men.

In his second monologue, Lélio resolves to live for his art. Inspired by the ghost in *Hamlet*, he imagines music sung by the dead (a unison chorus). As he speaks his final lines, a throbbing rhythm and strange harmonies set the scene. This movement is associated with both of the Shakespeare plays in which Berlioz saw Smithson acting. It is a revision of the 'Méditation' from his 1829 Prix de Rome cantata, *Cléopâtre*, and on the autograph

Berlioz wrote Juliet's words as she imagines herself waking, like Lélio, from a drugged sleep.[5] For the mélologue, Berlioz replaced Cleopatra's words with an invented nonsense language, which in turn he later replaced with French, having in the meantime used similar gibberish for the demons in *La Damnation*.

Lélio's third monologue begins as an invocation to Shakespeare, cursing detractors who considered him barbarous, and continues by denouncing those 'who dare to lend a hand to original works and subject them to horrible mutilations which they call *corrections* and *improvements*' (alluding to Fétis and Beethoven symphonies); Berlioz compares them to feral pigeons relieving themselves on statues of the gods, 'preening themselves as if they had laid a golden egg'.[6] This leads to a wild determination to have done with society and its routine-bound artistic establishment, obsessed with rules and good taste. Lélio declares he would rather live among outlaws: cue for a chorus of brigands with solo baritone. Its exact date of composition is uncertain; the words are Berlioz's, but the music may have been adapted from his lost setting, a year or two earlier, of words by either Hugo or Ferrand.[7] This rambunctious piece is remarkable for its daring harmony and rhythm, suited to the abandonment of civilized decorum: the brigands carry off women and drink their health from the skulls of their murdered lovers.[8]

The next two monologues are shorter. Lélio's thoughts turn to love; the solo tenor, representing Lélio himself rather than Horatio, sings his 'Chant de bonheur' ('Song of happiness'), adapted from the 1827 cantata *La Mort d'Orphée* and followed by a wistful echo of the melody, supposedly a shepherd trying to imitate Orpheus's singing; in *Lélio* this became 'The Aeolian harp. Memories'. Finally, Lélio resolves to work. The orchestra and chorus are revealed, ready to 'rehearse' (actually perform) Berlioz's *Fantaisie sur la Tempête de Shakespeare*, written in 1830, but after *Symphonie fantastique*. Although Lélio (the actor) does not conduct, he advises the performers on interpretation.

Berlioz composed *La Tempête* when betrothed to Camille Moke, whom he associated with Ariel. It opens with delicate 'Ariel' music – an early, if not the first, orchestral use of the piano – and portrays other characters from the play, ending with a vigorous coda. Here the 'mélologue' originally ended. In the revised version Lélio returns to thank the musicians; they start to leave but a few remain to play the opening of the *idée fixe*. 'Again!' cries Lélio, suddenly heartstricken; 'Again, and for ever' ('Encore, et pour toujours'). This melancholy ending binds the *mélologue* more closely to the symphony than was the case in 1832.

The mixture of music and speech makes *Lélio* hard to programme. Yet it can be surprisingly effective in performance, and the monologues contribute to our understanding of Berlioz's aesthetic principles. Apart from interventions of the *idée fixe*, all the music can be extracted and played on its own or in its original context. Like *Le Pêcheur*, the brigands' scene was published separately (before *Lélio* itself). The ghostly 'Méditation' in *La Mort de Cléopâtre* is now heard more often within its original context, as the cantata is a fine vehicle for a dramatic mezzosoprano. The two movements from *La Mort d'Orphée* are also very effective in their original form, though Berlioz added a magical finishing touch to the 'Aeolian harp' when revising *Lélio*. A chord builds up as if breezes are stirring the strings, producing natural overtones up to the seventh harmonic; the resulting dominant seventh is left unresolved. As for *La Tempête*, it is quite simply a symphonic poem *avant la lettre*.

Other Composers

The output of Berlioz's contemporaries contains very little that resembles *Symphonie fantastique*. In the 1830 Prix de Rome competition Édouard Millault (1808–87), also a student of Le Sueur, won second prize. He remained in Paris (as a violinist he probably played for Berlioz), and composed titled overtures and an orchestral fantasy, *La Mer* (*The Sea*); this, like *La Tempête*, is in four titled sections, one of them a storm. Millault's neoclassical 1835 symphony was not performed until 1871.The symphonies of Berlioz's near-contemporary Schubert were practically unknown even in Vienna. Those of the Swedish composer Franz Berwald (1796–68) and Berlioz's most distinguished French near-contemporary Louise Farrenc (1804–75) were composed after Berlioz's four. Berwald shares Berlioz's' fantastique' quality, notably in *Symphonie singulière* (1845). Farrenc's symphonies owe more to Mendelssohn, like those of younger German composers such as Emilie Mayer; powerfully expressive without the need for a programme. Mayer, however, like Wagner, composed a *Faust* overture. A symphonic tradition more postclassical than romantic, and hence a potential stick with which to beat Berlioz, is found in Gounod; in Bizet and Saint-Saëns as teenagers; perhaps in Brahms. All of these, however, appreciated Berlioz's music to some extent.

Francesca Brittan has unearthed two symphonies titled 'Fantastic' that followed closely upon Berlioz's. One, started as early as 1833 but later revised, was by a young Belgian, Jean-Étienne Soubre (1813–71); it even quotes Berlioz's work.[9] The other (1835) was by Berlioz's acquaintance François-Laurent-Hébert Turbry (1795–1859), whose music Fétis described in similar terms to those he applied to Berlioz: 'bizarre, erratic, disordered in ideas and their organization'.[10] Other composers affected by Berlioz's symphony did not attempt to compete on the same ground.

First was Liszt, who attended the premiere and the 1832 performance. His transcription of the symphony was published in 1834 as Op. 4, although the published orchestral score (1845) became Op. 14.[11] (Berlioz's opus numbers are not in order of composition; his true Op. 4 is the *King Lear* overture of 1831, published in 1840, before the symphony). Liszt's first creative response was to use themes from *Lélio* in a *Grande Fantaisie symphonique* for piano and orchestra (1835); he played the piano solo in this at a concert conducted by Girard, and Berlioz in his capacity as journalist wrote a favourable review. Berlioz conducted the fantasy himself the following year (18 December 1836) in a mixed programme including other works of his own and pieces by contemporary Italians, with Liszt also playing his transcription of 'Un bal' and 'Marche au supplice' from *Symphonie fantastique*.[12]

Liszt, noted for piety, was not claimed to be in league with the devil like his model in virtuosity, Paganini, but his evocations of the demonic in his *Mephisto* waltzes and *Faust Symphony* are unsurpassed even by Berlioz. His transformation technique, by which the 'Mephistopheles' movement in the symphony has no original themes but parodies those of the 'Faust' movement, is evidently indebted to Berlioz's 'Songe d'une nuit de Sabbat' even apart from the oblique homage at the opening (see Ex. 8.1). The *Faust* symphony was dedicated to Berlioz, who had earlier dedicated *La Damnation de Faust* to Liszt. A member of Liszt's circle, Joachim Raff (1822–82), encountered Berlioz on his visits to Weimar; some impact from Berlioz has been noted by Christopher Fifield.[13] When Liszt conducted a revival of *Benvenuto Cellini* (1852), Raff composed a virtuosic piano fantasia on some of its themes. His symphonic works are generally more cautious, reflecting his admiration of Mendelssohn, with whom he had hoped to study, but most of his symphonies have titles; the fifth (1872) is *Lenore*, named after the ballad by Gottfried Bürger in which a devil disguised as Lenore's dead lover carries her on horseback to the grave. The poem had been impressively set to music nearly seventy years earlier by Berlioz's future counterpoint teacher, Reicha; it later inspired a symphonic poem by Henri Duparc.

Berlioz's other concert-hall works offered different models of freedom from the conventions of genre. In *Harold en Italie* (1834) one theme, like the *idée fixe*, appears in every movement, but Berlioz distanced it from the *Fantastique*: rather than the centre of a drama, the protagonist is an observer, represented by the theme and the solo viola (although it is a symphony, not a viola concerto).[14] *Roméo et Juliette* (1839) is a choral symphony, but owes little to Beethoven's Ninth; after the sung programme (Prologue), it selects scenes from the play to illustrate mainly by instrumental music, with a funeral procession (a chorus; the scene is not in Shakespeare) and an operatic finale. There is no *idée fixe*, but there are dramatically motivated cross-references between movements.

Whereas Berlioz's Shakespearean lovers do not sing, in *La Damnation de Faust* (1846), conceived as a 'concert opera', and the oratorio *L'Enfance du Christ* (1854), the characters sing and the published scores include stage directions. *Roméo*, 'dramatic symphony', and *La Damnation*, 'dramatic legend', offered models for the creative mixture of musical genres hinted at by *Symphonie fantastique*. The term 'Ode-symphony', adopted by Félicien David's evocation of the Middle East, *Le Désert* (1844), takes a lead from Berlioz's works of mixed genre without reflecting much musical influence. Berlioz reacted with annoyance to those who thought his critical approval was because 'David is sailing in my wake', so evidently he saw the connection to his own work; he conducted a later performance.[15] He also reviewed favourably a 'Symphonie orientale' with voices, *Le Sélam* (1850) by Ernest Reyer.[16] Bizet evoked Davidian exoticism in the slow movement of his youthful Symphony in C (1855; unheard until the 1930s), and applied the term 'Ode-Symphonie' to his unfinished *Vasco de Gama* (1860).

As a symphonic device, the main use for recurring themes before *Symphonie fantastique* was in opera. This means of communicating something extramusical had been tried out long before Wagner's *Leitmotiv* by J.-B. Lemoine, Méhul, and Weber. In symphonies, the reprise of the Scherzo in the finale of Beethoven's Fifth is not really a precedent, although it may have encouraged Berlioz to experiment. The concept of a 'motto' in a symphony without a programme came later; mottos are usually short figures or progressions rather than a long melody like the *idée fixe*. However, Berlioz's concept contributed to the general trend towards a more overt type of coherence (or 'unity') that theorists (perhaps also composers) came to desire: symphonies, expressive of emotions explicit or impalpable, were to be experienced as wholes greater than the sum of their parts, whereas in earlier periods movements of works in the same key could be, and sometimes were, interchangeable. Examples of the uses of recurring themes or mottoes could be multiplied in symphonies by later composers such as Schumann, Bruckner, Brahms, Elgar, Mahler, and Debussy in his 'symphonic sketches', *La Mer*.

The effect of *Symphonie fantastique* can be felt in other genres as, along with overtures by Mendelssohn and Berlioz himself, it provided a stimulus for concert works with evocative titles though not always, or even usually, with a programme handed to the audience. This type of music, following Liszt's lead, is usually called a symphonic poem, and like Berlioz's *La Tempête* is an uninterrupted piece incorporating changes of tempo and character. An egregious example is *Macbeth* by a British composer who settled in Germany, Henry Hugo Pierson; the music follows the action more closely than Berlioz ever did, with lines from the play (in German translation) entered into the published score.[17] The dimensions of the symphonic poem swelled to those of a symphony; César Franck's *Psyché* (1888) is a dramatic symphony with chorus, with an orchestral love scene (like *Roméo et Juliette*). One of Berlioz's later admirers, Richard Strauss, wrote symphonic poems, but called his two last big programmatic works symphonies, one domestic, one alpine.

Symphonie fantastique was a major factor in liberating the musical imaginations of later romantic composers. Berlioz's inclusion of theatrical elements (offstage oboe and bells; the concealed orchestra when *Lélio* is performed) is probably less significant than his use of instruments not usually employed in symphonies: piccolo, cor anglais, ophicleide, E♭ clarinet, and unpitched percussion. In addition to his enlargement of orchestral forces, mentioned earlier, Beethoven provided another precedent for the *haute vulgarisation* of 'Marche au supplice'; the finale of his Ninth Symphony includes a march, in 6/8 and popular in style, like Berlioz's 6/8 chorus of soldiers in *Huit scènes de Faust* rather than grotesque. Beethoven's trombone parts reflect the instrument's nobility, even perhaps its earlier association with the church rather than the concert hall. The shrill E♭ clarinet, or the slightly larger D clarinet, returned to the expanded symphony orchestra of Mahler and Strauss, notably at the execution of the eponymous prankster in the latter's *Till Eulenspiegels lustige Streiche*.

Other musical resources such as combination of themes also originated in opera rather than symphonies, although, again, Beethoven's Ninth provides a precedent in the finale (from bar 655). In 1830 Berlioz had not yet heard the Ninth, but he must have studied the score prior to his first essay on Beethoven (1829); he describes the 'reunion of themes' in his later study of the symphonies.[18]

Berlioz enlarged the repertoire of topics that could be used in symphonies. Tchaikovsky's Sixth, the *Pathétique*, has a waltz (but in quintuple metre) and a march, though the latter topic was relatively common, sharing with the Minuet and Contredanse symphonic regions that evoke movement. However, symphonic march tempi, like the finale of Beethoven's Fifth, are not usually *headed* 'March', still less 'March to Execution'. The 'learned style' of strict counterpoint and fugue appears in many earlier symphonies, with fugato a significant feature of Beethoven's *Eroica*, Seventh, and Ninth, but this sort of counterpoint is usually reserved for graver music than Berlioz's finale.

What is probably the newest element, apart from the programme, is the grotesque: not just in the distortion of the *idée fixe* but in such details as the bassoon counterpoints and juxtaposition of G minor and D♭ in the March. The 'Wolf's Glen' in Weber's *Der Freischütz* provided Berlioz with an example of truly eerie music, and the remarkable orchestral reminiscence of an earlier scene when peasants mocked the hero, Max, anticipates Berlioz's mockery of the *idée fixe* and *Dies irae*. In 1829 Berlioz had composed a chorus of ghosts (*Ballet des ombres*, published as Op. 2 but withdrawn and surviving by chance). The piano accompaniment to this ghostly dance invites orchestration; it makes free use of dissonance, and its first bar is a transposed version of the discord that opens the finale of Beethoven's Ninth. The voices are required to glissando over small intervals and before a short piano coda their parts end on a chord of D♭ superimposed on a bass C.

The topic sometimes identified as 'hymn' (slow moving, homophonic) is suggested at the end of the first movement, but was hardly a novelty. Nor was plainchant new to the symphony, although Berlioz was probably unaware of its use, for instance, by Haydn. Even if he knew Mozart's last symphony ('Jupiter') he might not have identified the four-note motive (the first of five fugue subjects in the finale) as connected to plainchant.

In contrast to Mendelssohn's introduction of a chorale into the *Reformation Symphony*, Berlioz's use of plainchant is frankly blasphemous. It is unclear to what extent his burlesque of the *Dies irae* could be counted as an influence on citations of the same chant in instrumental works by later composers, at least when their subject matter justified the reference. His pianist contemporaries used it: Valentin Alkan in 'Morte', implying the death of a woman (Op. 15 no 3, 1837), Chopin in his ostensibly non-referential *Préludes* Op. 28 (1838–9), overtly in No. 2, elsewhere disguised.[19] Neither of these composers had much time for

Berlioz's music, unlike Liszt, who used the chant in *Totentanz* (death-dance, 1849). Berlioz's younger colleague Saint-Saëns introduced it in *Danse macabre* (1874), although only in a satirical jig-like form; like the 'Ronde du Sabbat', this short symphonic poem includes a fugal passage and a combination of themes.

There seems no obvious reason for the startling appearance of the *Dies irae* in Tchaikovsky's Third Orchestral Suite (Op. 55); during the long finale it breaks into Variation 4 like the fate theme in the mostly joyous finale of his Fourth Symphony. When Rachmaninoff conducted *Symphonie fantastique* in Moscow in 1912 he had already used the *Dies irae* for the obvious reason in his tone poem *The Isle of the Dead* (1909). Nikolai Myaskovsky introduced it into his sixth symphony (completed 1923), a lament for those killed in war and revolution. In Rachmaninoff's *Rhapsody on the Theme of Paganini* (1934), as in Tchaikovsky's suite, the chant intrudes on a mostly genial set of variations. Eugène Ysaÿe used it in all four movements of his second sonata for unaccompanied violin; the movements are headed 'Obsession', 'Melancholy', 'Dance of ghosts', and 'The Furies'. Less obviously motivated is its appearance in Ottorino Respighi's depiction of a Brazilian snake farm (*Impressioni brasiliane*, 1928), though the intention may again be satirical.

Notes

1 Richard Taruskin, *The Oxford History of Western Music*, Vol. 3 *Music in the Nineteenth Century* (New York: Oxford University Press, 2005), 318–40.

2 Holoman, *Berlioz*, 624.

3 'Le programme suivant doit être distribué à l'auditoire toutes les fois que la symphonie fantastique est exécutée dramatiquement et suivie, en conséquence, du monodrame de Lélio, qui termine et complète *l'épisode de la vie d'un artiste*. En pareil cas, l'orchestre invisible est disposé sur la scène d'un théâtre derrière la toile baissée.' NBE 16, 170.

4 Letter to Albert du Boys, 4–5 March 1832; *CG* I, 535–7 (cited, 536).

5 *Romeo and Juliet*, Act IV scene 3. Facsimile of the first page: NBE 6, 232.

6 '... qui osent porter la main sur ouvrages originaux, leur font subir d'horribles mutilations qu'ils s'appellent *Corrections* et *perfection- nements*, pour lesquels, disent-ils, il faut *beaucoup de goût*. ... se pavannent fiers et satisfaits comme s'ils venaient de pondre un œuf d'or'. Berlioz, *Lélio* (ed. Peter Bloom), NBE 7 (Kassel: Bärenreiter, 1992), 23.

7 Berlioz, *Lélio* (NBE 7), XI–XII.

8 Analysis in Julian Rushton, *The Musical Language of Berlioz*, 14–22.

9 Jean-Étienne-Joseph Soubre, *Sinfonie fantastique*, Critical Edition, ed. Francesca Brittan (Madison, WI: A-R Editions, 2017); see the Preface and Brittan's PhD thesis 'Berlioz, Hoffmann, and the *Genre fantastique* in French Romanticism' (PhD dissertation, Cornell University, 2007).

10 *CG*, Vol. I, 199n.

11 *Episode de la vie d'un Artiste. Grande symphonie fantastique* par Hector Berlioz, œuv: 4me. Partition de Piano par F. Liszt (Paris: Schlesinger, 1834).

12 Holoman, *Berlioz*, 614.

13 Christopher Fifield, *The German Symphony between Beethoven and Brahms:The Fall and Rise of a Genre* (Farnham: Ashgate, 2015), 99–100, 206–8.

14 *Memoirs*, chap. 45.

15 Letter to his sister Nancy Pal, 1 January 1845. *CG* Vol. 9 (*Nouvelles Lettres*), 253.

16 Berlioz, *Critique musicale* Vol. 7, 281.

17 Julian Rushton, 'Henry Hugo Pierson and Shakesperean Tragedy', in Rachel Cowgill and Julian Rushton (eds.), *Europe, Empire and Spectacle in Nineteenth-Century British Music* (Aldershot: Ashgate, 2006), 77–95.

18 *À travers chants*, 60; (ed. Guichard), 77.

19 Anatole Leikin, *The Mystery of Chopin's Préludes* (Farnham: Ashgate, 2015), 53–66. See also Robin Gregory, '*Dies irae*', *Music & Letters* 34 (1953): 133–9; Malcolm Boyd, 'Dies Irae: Some Recent Manifestations', *Music & Letters* 49 (1968): 347–56.

RECEPTION

Schumann and Musical Form

It would require a whole book adequately to cover nearly 200 years of conflicting opinions about *Symphonie fantastique*. It was not widely reviewed before Berlioz went to Italy and the early reviews are of relatively little interest for modern study of the work.[1] The real story began because the composer Robert Schumann, also editor of the Leipzig *Neue Zeitschrift für Musik*, corresponded with musicians and critics in Paris to inform his readers about developments there. He published French reviews in translation, and in June 1835 he himself wrote about Berlioz. After this he published the critical article by François-Joseph Fétis, and followed it with his own lengthy review, spread over several issues (articles in the *Neue Zeitschrift* were each only a few pages long).[2]

Schumann's evaluation of *Symphonie fantastique* is generally positive, though perhaps affected by misinformation: he knew of Berlioz's infatuation with a 'British' woman (Smithson), and of his medical studies, but wrongly supposed that he came from Northern France and had composed the work in 1820. Yet Fétis's 1835 article mentions meeting Berlioz 'about twelve years ago': more likely nine years ago, as he refers to an inept counterpoint exercise, probably Berlioz's fugue that failed the preliminary test for the Prix de Rome in 1826. Fétis's comments motivated Schumann to make a thorough investigation through the prism of Liszt's 'partition de piano'. When he republished the review in his collected writings, he made minor revisions that suggest a more cautious evaluation; by then he had actually heard the symphony in Dresden. As Hugh Macdonald remarks, these composers' relationship 'was at its closest in the years 1835 to 1837, before they ever met'; their later personal contact was hampered by neither being fluent in the other's language.[3]

The First Movement as Sonata Form

Sonata form has been the subject of definitions at least since Reicha laid out a scheme he called 'large binary form' ('grande coupe binaire'): a movement in two parts, both repeated.[4] This definition, good for most of the previous half-century or more, was eroded when the second repeat was abandoned (e.g. by Beethoven). An alternative ternary layout is implied by listing the main sections: exposition (repeated), development, and recapitulation (not repeated); this has the advantage of being applicable when the exposition is not repeated, as in overtures.

Within these general frameworks, some theorists have emphasized the key scheme as the defining factor: themes P and S exposed respectively in the tonic and a complementary key (usually the dominant) and recapitulated with both themes in the tonic, resolving a large-scale tonal dissonance. Alternatively, analysts have defined the form by themes, which are more likely to be perceived by listeners and so to govern their reactions; in my teaching experience, this is the version of sonata form that students are most likely to recognize.

The twentieth century produced other criteria for signposting longer movements. Heinrich Schenker's theory, resisting the concept of modulation (key change), connects everything to a two-part fundamental structure (*Ursatz*), the upper part the descending 'fundamental line' (*Urlinie*). From the point of view of perception, and considering the individual points of interest in larger forms, this can be problematic, even with movements less free-ranging than Berlioz's.

More promising for sonata forms is a combination of a key scheme with thematic 'rotation' and noting the variations from one or other template. Schumann used just such a template – the 'traditional model' against which he measured the first-movement Allegro of *Symphonie fantastique*. Departures from a template are sometimes termed 'deformation', but this is more a sign of originality than a defect. Recent studies have multiplied the template subspecies, but this hardly concerns us in connection with Berlioz's 'deformation', if that is what it is, or his possible understanding of the sonata forms of predecessors such as Mozart, Reicha, or Beethoven.[5]

Sonata form has long been in some danger of being over-theorized, with emphasis on taxonomy rather than on the special qualities of individual movements. Such emphasis leads to dissent about Berlioz, largely focused on the first-movement Allegro of *Symphonie fantastique*. Macdonald is bold enough to suggest that it 'has little in common with classical sonata form'.[6] Certainly it is not, in Reicha's sense, binary, and the rearrangement of themes after the repeated exposition shakes up conventional notions of development–retransition–recapitulation (see Table 4.2). Yet it is possible to find it at least relatively orthodox as a reinterpretation of the 'grande coupe'.

I concluded in an earlier study that it is 'a capricious form appropriate to its subject, obeying its own laws'.[7] Maybe 'fantasies' would have been better than 'laws', and perhaps the Allegro works best if its programme is borne in mind as we listen: a loving reverie disturbed by darker passions. But this is still Berlioz's creative response to sonata forms by his immediate predecessors. Even before becoming acquainted with overtures by Beethoven, he knew how to shape such pieces (*Les Francs-juges* and *Waverley*) on lines compatible with those of Cherubini, Rossini, or Weber: slow section, sonata action, coda. If he had not decided to repeat the exposition in *Symphonie fantastique* (an afterthought), it might have seemed less like a symphonic first movement and more like a long overture such as his own *King Lear*.

There are other ways of perceiving the Allegro. In his analysis ('Schumann Amplified'), Edward T. Cone took Schumann's symmetrical diagram of the whole movement (including the Largo) as a starting point, implicitly accepting his predecessor's conclusion that in relation to standard definitions 'in terms of variety and uniformity', the 'traditional model' has no claim to superiority over Berlioz's form; Schumann modestly adds: 'We only wish we possessed a truly colossal imagination and could then pursue it wherever it goes.'[8] He compared his interpretation with his

Table 10.1 *Schumann's outline of Berlioz's Allegro and the 'traditional model'*

Berlioz				
		P		
	Middle, with S theme		Middle, with S theme	
P (*idée fixe*)				S, P (C major)
C major	G major, E minor	G major	E minor, G major	C major
'Traditional model'				
Exposition: P	S: end of exposition	Development	Recapitulation of P	Recapitulation of S (coda)
C major	G major	A minor	C major	C major

'traditional model' in two superimposed tables (ignoring the exposition repeat); these are represented in Table 10.1, using the symbols of Table 4.2.

On a row below the Berlioz version, omitted from Table 10.1, Schumann wrote 'Beginning C major' and 'Close C major', with *Anfang* ('beginning') well to the left of the P theme (see Figure 10.1). This suggests that the Largo and the closing stages (coda) are the foundation of an arch form, with the G major *idée fixe* at its apex. But to support the arch on the Largo and coda is unconvincing; the Largo is far longer, uses different themes, and has no role in the discussion of sonata forms on Schumann's 'traditional model'. Schumann probably intended his comparison to cover only the Allegro, and Cone, interpreting Schumann's 'beginning' as the Largo, duly notes that it is actually in C minor. Otherwise, for the Allegro, Cone usefully elaborates Schumann's arch.[9]

Schumann wisely adds that Berlioz does not 'squeeze the last drop out of his themes; nor does he stifle a good idea under tedious thematic development'.[10] In so far as sections are defined by themes, Cone feels it appropriate to refer to 'ambiguity', and it is surely permissible, and not an aesthetic weakness, for listeners

Figure 10.1 Schumann's table of the first-movement form. From 'Hector Berlioz, *Episode de la vie d'un Artiste. Grande Symphonie fantastique . . .*', *NZfM* (July–August 1835), issues 10–13

(even for analysts) to identify the music's formal signposts differently. Cone takes the passage that leads to the recapitulation (from bar 358, his 360) as a transition. Yet it is so strongly characterized by the oboe solo, heard above motifs from the *idée fixe*, that it might better be considered a developmental episode. Cone locates the coda at bar 475 (his 477) because of the massive 'perfect authentic' cadence (PAC: bass G–C, C in the treble). True, the

PAC coincides with completion of a typical 'Urlinie', with its descent to the tonic (E–D–C) covered by the violins' high G; traditional theories would support this choice. However, the 'sense of an ending' is perceptible earlier, at the *animez* with its twofold interruption of C major by B7 (439, 461); this music is not recapitulating anything heard earlier, apart from the wistful reminiscence of the *idée fixe* that interrupts these interruptions. Thus I prefer to consider that Berlioz decided to merge climactic recapitulation, peroration, and coda; precise identification of the starting point of the coda seems relatively unimportant.

Reasonably enough, Cone classifies the Allegro as a sonata form with 'exceptions': the G major *idée fixe* and the early reprise of S. He considers the oboe solo episode a flaw since 'the music has to be set in motion again', although such fluctuations of mood and motion surely befit a movement headed 'rêveries, passions'. Cone concludes that 'it is hard to make sense of this either as an academically "correct" sonata form or as the prolongation of a single controlling progression', but as a true musician he also wrote 'somehow the movement always works in performance'.[11] Which, surely, is what matters most.

That Berlioz fits awkwardly with theoretical positions not fully formulated in 1830 is hardly surprising, and could be considered a weakness of later theory rather than of his music. Carl Dahlhaus compares Schubert's and Berlioz's sonata forms sympathetically, adding that it 'is idle to speculate whether the themes in the recapitulation appear in reverse order, or whether we are dealing with a relic of the Baroque suite' (the latter reference – to what? binary dance movements? – was perhaps intended ironically). Dahlhaus credits Berlioz with taking 'one of Beethoven's principles to solve a problem unknown to Beethoven', finding his own path on the premise that 'large-scale symphonic form emerges from the relation between monumentality and sophisticated thematic manipulation'.[12] Reviewing Schumann and Cone, Fred Everett Maus shrewdly notes that Schumann compared Berlioz's design to the 'traditional model' not to suggest that one derived from the other but rather to emphasize Berlioz's originality. Maus pays due attention to the first of Schumann's articles, purportedly by Schumann's *fantastique* alter ego, 'Florestan'; the remainder he signed himself, referring to Florestan as if he were a different person. Schumann's analysis, Maus points out that Schumann's analysis, unlike most of his critical writings, 'speaks a language that we still use'.[13]

Using the theory of rotation and taking into account more than design engineering, Stephen Rodgers's chapter headed 'The *vague des passions*, monomania, and the first movement of the *Symphonie fantastique*' is a thoughtful discussion of the first movement.[14] Following discussion of sources of the programme, he takes 'a broad view' of the form, 'exploring how it combines rotational and sonata principles as well as how the *idée fixe* changes'. He points to the *idée fixe* as 'the impulse that sets these waves in motion', referring to 'multiple waves' (with both implications of 'vague'; see Chapter 3). He tabulates the 'rotations' of P and S themes, with TR for transition and X for other ideas initiated by the *idée fixe* (bars 72, 166, 232, 410, 503).[15] Cone's 'flaw' is registered as transition ('TR', 291) and 'X/P' (358), X being the oboe solo, P the *idée fixe*, which at this point does not initiate a rotation as it does from bar 166. He later refers to this section as 'the retransition theme', another reflection of the unusual nature of the passage, since sonata retransitions, preparing the recapitulation, do not usually have their own themes.[16]

Rodgers well reflects the nature of a movement in which formal divisions are susceptible of different, even multiple interpretations, and he asks, most pertinently, why Berlioz references 'the conventions of sonata form?' while distorting them 'to heighten the form's circularity'. If this sounds as if Berlioz had studied rotation theory (he is not actually known to have studied even Reicha's theory), I am perhaps to blame, as Rodgers cites my comment that any perceived inadequacy 'could be the result of a wrong reading rather than any flaw in music which possesses conviction even in its composed hesitations'.[17] Rodgers's analysis deserves to be read as a whole; it accommodates Schumann and Cone and other recent analyses such as those by Christian Berger and Wolfgang Dömling. And he has the gift of striking expression; the apex of Schumann's arch is 'a curious circus-carousel variant of the *idée fixe* that hollows out the form and calls into question conventional notions of development and recapitulation'.[18] Which seems exactly right.

Let us, therefore, leave the sonata form, ambiguous in relationship to the 'traditional model' and to 'rotation' but nevertheless convincing in performance. Whatever Berlioz thought he was doing, he reconfigured elements both traditional and original to suit his purposes: a singing melody (*idée fixe*) as the P theme, both connected to and separated from the S theme, developing its first phrase and P2 separately, and transforming its character at the recapitulation before partly restoring it in the wistful, fragmentary coda.

Other Formal and Stylistic Elements

Cone also applies an analytical method associated with Arnold Schönberg and expounded by Rudolph Réti that aims to uncover connections between disparate themes.[19] A starting point is the semitone motif shared by the Florian song and the *idée fixe* (see brackets in Ex. 4.1 and 4.3). An episode in 'Un Bal' (from 78) adapts the semitone to the waltz rhythm, with a tonal outcome: the upper note (C♮) is held at bar 116 to prepare for the *idée fixe* in F. Semitones permeate the finale, as when the fugue breaks down (from 279). Such thematic connections, in theory, relate principal themes to episodic and even apparently athematic passages, lending coherence to a work that glories in diversity. This semitone motif is only really convincing as an element in the work's 'unity' when followed by the same motivic shape covering a whole tone; this happens in the *idée fixe*, then in 'Scène aux champs' (38–41) and at the very end of the symphony (Ex. 8.6).

Rodgers, without referencing Wotton's comment, finds tenuous connections between the *idée fixe* and the first-movement oboe solo.[20] But the elements isolated by him and Cone are the Lego bricks of large-scale tonal structures; however much, or little, they affect perception of the finished work, it is unlikely that they figured in Berlioz's creative process (which is not to deny their existence). In search of an overarching design, Cone compares the outer movements, and finds implications of 'ambiguity' with sonata-form associations that he uncovers within the March and the finale. But aesthetically, even without a programme, symphonies do not stand or fall by such matters, largely imperceptible in performance.

Schumann found points to criticize, and in dismissing the finale he is scarcely kinder than Fétis. 'Florestan' ended Schumann's first article by referring to Berlioz's 'destructive rage ... the music also encloses his dreams and his attempted suicide in an embrace hateful and crude. The bells toll for that, and skeletons at the organ strike up the wedding dance. ... At this point the spirit [of art] turns away from him weeping'.[21] This only partly corresponds to the programme, of which Schumann disapproved in principle; he says Beethoven need not have named his Sixth Symphony 'Pastoral', as its nature is clear to the listener (nevertheless he named his own first and third symphonies 'Spring' and 'Rhenish'). Beethoven's pastoral topics (running water, birdsong, merrymaking, *tempesta*, alphorn) were not new; Berlioz used some of them in 'Scène aux champs' and other traditional topics elsewhere: religion (I and V), waltz, march, learned style, parody.[22] And despite the fame, or infamy, of the finale, the mood swings of the first movement – Largo and Allegro – are no less strikingly original.

Schumann excoriated Fétis for asserting that Berlioz lacked harmonic invention, his damning conclusion being that this theorist and scholar of early music suffered 'sheer blindness, a complete lack of feeling for this kind of music'.[23] But even Schumann was perturbed by the G-minor and D♭ juxtaposition at the climax of the March. This also annoyed Schenker, who otherwise paid little attention to Berlioz; in his 1906 *Harmonielehre* he quoted Schumann's reference to 'awkwardness', but he read the passage as ♭II–v in C minor, where V, to be functional, should be major. Hence Schenker concluded, gratuitously, 'a true D♭ major' is impossible here.[24] Berlioz intended no such thing, and only a convoluted mind would try to parse the passage in C minor.

By contrast, Leonard G. Ratner calls this tritone juxtaposition 'one of the most arresting progressions in the entire romantic literature .... The entire passage brings the grotesquerie of this movement to a frenzied culmination'.[25] Programmatically, in his nightmare we may imagine the protagonist (D♭) struggling with guards dragging him to the guillotine, which falls in G minor (169); musically, the chordal juxtaposition is an outcome of an earlier passage (from 122) where the main theme in G minor is followed by its inversion in D♭. Schenker, quoting only bars 152–7, does not mention this, nor

129

Berlioz's conflict resolution by what Cone calls his 'typical device of progressive reinterpretation: the D♭ (C#) is retained in the flutes while the harmonies containing it constantly change'. Cone compares this passage to the first-movement Largo where 'progressive reinterpretation' of A♭ as G# breaks through into the C-major Allegro (see Ex. 4.2).[26]

Ratner reminds us of the vital role of song and 'Berlioz's eccentric handling of sound and figure' that creates 'the "hostile" environment' for the Florian song.[27] The accompaniments of this and the *idée fixe*, rather than supporting the melodies, tend to destabilize them. Given the programme, this hardly justifies Ratner's epithet 'eccentric', except in so far as Berlioz is literally outside the once-perceived 'centre' or mainstream usually equated with Haydn, Mozart, Beethoven and, perhaps more problematically in some respects, Schubert. On harmonization, Schumann gave Berlioz the benefit of the doubt: 'One has only to try adjusting things here and there, improving them a little – as is child's play for anyone well versed in harmony! – to discover instead how lacklustre and insipid the result!'[28] Attempts to do this, by Ratner and myself, tend to confirm this insight; to establish a more 'normal' harmonic rhythm, Berlioz's unequal phrase lengths have to be adjusted, draining the melody of much of its character.[29] This is perhaps the reason that even today there are those who deny Berlioz the ability to write a 'tune', whereas others find his music rich in melodic beauty. Let Schumann have the last word:

M. Fétis contends that not even Berlioz's dearest friends would dare to defend him on the question of *melody*. If this be so, then I plainly belong to the enemy camp. But let us not think in terms of Italian melody – the sort that we know perfectly even before it starts.[30]

Notes

1. Peter Bloom lists *Le National* (6 December), *Le Figaro* (7 December), *Revue musicale* (11 December), *Le Correspondant* (14 December), *Le Temps* (26 December), and *La Revue de Paris* (December). 'Berlioz in the Year of the *Symphonie fantastique*', 24. Bloom discusses these reviews in '"Politics" and the Musical Press in 1830', *Periodica Musica* 5 (1987), 9–16.

2. Robert Schumann, 'Ueber Berlioz und seine Compositionen', *Neue Zeitschrift für Musik* (June 1835), issues 17, 18. François-Joseph Fétis, in *La Revue musicale* (1 February 1835), translated as 'Fétis über Hector Berlioz und dessen Symphonie', *NZfM* (June 1835), issues 49, 50; English translation: Cone, *Fantastic Symphony*, 215–20. Schumann, '"Aus dem Leben eines Künstlers": Phantastische Symphonie in 5 Abtheilungen von Hector Berlioz', *NZfM* (July 1835), 9; 'Hector Berlioz, *Episode de la vie d'un Artiste. Grande Symphonie fantastique* ...', *NZfM* (July–August 1835), issues 10–13; English translations: Cone, *Fantastic Symphony*, 221–48 and Bent (ed.), *Music Analysis in the Nineteenth Century*, Vol. II, 161–94. Both Cone and Bent take note of what Schumann changed or omitted in his *Gesammelte Schriften* (Leipzig: Georg Wigands Verlag, 1854), 118–51.

3. 'Berlioz and Schumann', in Hugh Macdonald, *Beethoven's Century* (Rochester, NY: University of Rochester Press, 2008), 42–56; cited, 42.

4. Antoine Reicha, *Traité de haute composition musicale* (Paris: Zetter & Cie, 1824–5).

5. Sonata theory prior to the twenty-first century is expertly summarized by James Webster: 'Sonata Form', in Stanley Sadie and John Tyrrell (eds.), *The New Grove Dictionary of Music and Musicians* (London: Macmillan, 2001), Vol. 23, 687–701 (www .oxfordmusiconline.com/grovemusic/view/10.1093/gmo/ 9781561592630.001.0001/omo-9781561592630-e-0000026197? goto=sonataform&pos=1&type=article). Heinrich Schenker's theories are expounded by Felix Salzer, *Structural Hearing:Tonal Coherence in Music* (New York: Dover, 1962). Newer ideas such as rotation are employed by James Hepokoski, *Sibelius: Symphony No. 5* (Cambridge: Cambridge University Press, 1991); see also James Hepokoski and Warren Darcy, *Elements of Sonata Theory: Norms, Types, and Deformations in the Late Eighteenth Century Sonata* (New York: Oxford University Press, 2006).

6. Hugh Macdonald, *Berlioz Orchestral Music* (London: BBC Publications, 1969), 34.

7. Julian Rushton, *The Musical Language of Berlioz*, 192, 274 n.94.

8. Bent, *Music Analysis in the Nineteenth Century* II, 175.

9. See Cone, *Fantastic Symphony*, 231 (Schumann); Cone's more elaborate arch, 252.

10. Bent, *Music Analysis in the Nineteenth Century* II, 181.

11. Edward T. Cone, 'Inside the Saint's Head: The Music of Berlioz', in *The Musical Newsletter* I–II (1971–2), reprinted in Cone, *Music: A View from Delft* (Chicago: University of Chicago Press, 1989), 217–48; cited, 223–4.

12. Carl Dahlhaus, *Nineteenth-Century Music*, trans. J. Bradford Robinson (Berkeley: University of California Press, 1989), 154–6; cited, 156.

13. Fred Everett Maus, 'Intersubjectivity and Analysis: Schumann's Essay on the *Fantastic Symphony*', in Ian Bent (ed.), *Music Theory in the Age of Romanticism* (Cambridge: Cambridge University Press, 1996), 125–37; cited, 125.

14. Stephen Rodgers, *Form, Program, and Metaphor in the Music of Berlioz* (Cambridge: Cambridge University Press, 2009), 85–106.

15. Rodgers, *Form, Program, and Metaphor*, 91–3.

16. Rodgers, *Form, Program, and Metaphor*, 101.

17. Rodgers, *Form, Program, and Metaphor*, 93; Rushton, *The Music of Berlioz*, 258.

18. Rodgers, *Form, Program, and Metaphor*, 95.

19. Cone, *Fantastic Symphony*, 253–76. Rudolph Réti, *The Thematic Process in Music* (New York: Macmillan, 1951).

20. Rodgers, *Form, Program, and Metaphor*, 101; Wotton, see Chapter 3 note 34 and Chapter 4, note 11.

21. Bent, *Music Analysis in the Nineteenth Century* II, 169.

22. See 'Topics' in CBE, 333–4, and Julian Horton, 'Listening to Topics in the Nineteenth century', Chapter 25 in Danuta Mirka (ed.), *The Oxford Handbook of Topic Theory* (New York: Oxford University Press, 2014); on *Symphonie fantastique*, 643–4.

23. Bent, *Music Analysis in the Nineteenth Century* II, 177–8.

24. Bent, *Music Analysis in the Nineteenth Century* II, 178. Heinrich Schenker, *Harmonielehre* (1906), rev. and annotated by Oswald Jonas and trans. Elizabeth Mann Borgese as *Harmony* (Chicago: University of Chicago Press, 1954), 112–13.

25. Leonard G. Ratner, *Romantic Music: Sound and Syntax* (New York: Schirmer, 1992), 111.

26. Cone, *Fantastic Symphony*, 269.

27. Ratner, *Romantic Music*, 197–208; cited, 198.

28. Bent, *Music Analysis in the Nineteenth Century* II, 180.

29. Ratner, *Romantic Music*, 208; Rushton, *The Musical Language of Berlioz* (on 'La belle voyageuse' from *Irish Melodies*), 63–6.

30. Bent, *Music Analysis in the Nineteenth Century* II, 187.

OTHER APPROACHES

Conclusion

The twentieth- and twenty-first-century literature on *Symphonie fantastique* is vast and varied, and interest in Berlioz is international; the New Berlioz Edition prints extensive introductory materials in English, French, and German, and his prose works are published in these and other languages. The perceived predominance of Anglo-American work on Berlioz may account for the fact that relatively few recent publications in other languages have been translated into English, although a certain amount of work by English authors has appeared in French, including David Cairns's outstanding biography. Its bulkiest French predecessor, by Adolphe Boschot, has not appeared in English and is now likely to be consulted only by specialists. This handbook is primarily addressed to those of whatever nationality who read English, but over the years I have derived benefit from work in French, German, and Italian, some of which is listed in the Bibliography. Since my 2001 book *The Music of Berlioz*, however, this has not greatly affected my thoughts on *Symphonie fantastique* (although I am prepared to admit the possibility that it should have).

I have mentioned the tendency to regard *Symphonie fantastique* as the key work in Berlioz's output, despite his other three symphonies, three complete operas (fascinating in themselves and for how little they have in common), three mature sacred works (Requiem, Te Deum, *L'Enfance du Christ*, as well as the interesting but immature *Messe solennelle*), and several songs and choruses often of great charm; some of the songs are among the finest of their time, notably *La Mort d'Ophélie* and the six songs of *Les Nuits d'été*.

Presumably if he had won the Prix de Rome (as he deserved) in 1828, the impact of Harriet Smithson, Shakespeare, and

Beethoven might have had a different outcome. He would prob-ably have spent longer in Italy, and a year in Germany as the prize required; this he successfully pleaded to be allowed to forego. He would have returned to Paris at about the same time, in 1832, but in that alternative history it would have been a different Hector Berlioz, one never engaged to Camille Moke and probably not the composer of *Symphonie fantastique*, let alone its sequel.

Recent developments in critical writing and musicology have viewed *Symphonie fantastique* from angles different from those mostly adopted in this handbook. Some of this work might be criticized for shying away from the actual notes (by which I mean the sound of the music as much as its notation). However, modern, or postmodern, viewpoints can reveal aspects of complex works like *Symphonie fantastique* by interrogating them in new ways. Problems arise less from evading analysis than from incorporating into the discussion what is ostensibly analysis but proves to be wrong as to the musical facts; but if even Schumann can err in that respect, it is hardly fair to expect every writer's engagement with the music to be free of error.

***

Berlioz's *Mémoires* established a biographical framework for his career that is true in essence if not in every detail. It has been modified where necessary by his biographers, sometimes (for instance, in Boschot's three volumes) with thinly veiled expres-sions of doubt about Berlioz's veracity. Most recent authors have accepted that his slips are lapses of memory, mostly trivial, rather than wilful attempts to rewrite history. Yet no autobiography can be entirely free of self-justification before the tribunal of posterity; in this respect Berlioz's reminiscences are no different from others, and more entertaining than most.

Recent attempts to fathom Berlioz's mentality and worldview have been no less productive for avoiding the framework of biography. Taking a lead from his childhood interest in maps and travel that (beyond Europe) he could never undertake, Inge van Rij discusses *Symphonie fantastique* under the heading 'Visions of Other Worlds: Sensing the Supernatural' in her chapter about the symphony, *Lélio*, and the unfinished opera *La Nonne sanglante*.

Although the programme represents, in whole or in part, a drug-induced nightmare, there is nothing actually supernatural about it; even 'Songe d'une nuit de Sabbat' is only a dream of something unreal. However, van Rij finds plenty to say, starting with the programme's visual dimension, although this is obscured when the symphony is coupled with *Lélio*.[1] She details novel entertainments of the period that depended on science – camera obscura, panorama, diorama, and others – that could have attracted the attention of a composer with a known interest in scientific matters. These conceivably affected his conception of *Symphonie fantastique*. Van Rij associates phantasmagoria with the 'Marche au supplice' and the concealed singers and orchestra of the *mélologue*. The kaleidoscope as analogy for Berlioz's 'polarity of timbre and instrumental colour' is well illustrated by the March (from 109) and finale (456–87). However, the thaumatrope, an optical toy that merges images, is less likely to have been a precedent for Berlioz's combinations of themes than actual music that had used a technique considerably older than these scientific gadgets. Equally suspect is the discussion of the division of violin sections in the first movement (see Ex. 2.2). Perhaps this does add an expressive bite to the passage (as van Rij puts it, the players are forced to 'spit out their fragments'), but it is not stereophonic even when the violins are correctly placed on either side of the conductor, as the sections, unlike in, say, a baroque trio sonata, are not exchanging material; so there seems no point in connecting the passage to the visual experience of the stereoscope.

Overall, van Rij's book, while it opens angles of approach only touched on by most recent work on Berlioz, either biographical or concerned with music analysis and criticism, needs to be approached with caution; it is as if a wide landscape is being studied through a small window with a certain amount of distortion in the glass. As I have suggested, this has relatively little effect on her study of *Symphonie fantastique*; however, her approach, a form of postmodern critical musicology, is over-eager to dismiss actual study of the musical workings, even within their known cultural context, as objects of analysis. One review suggests that her concern with criticizing the political culture of an era of imperialism and colonialism leads to some odd conclusions. One such is a perspective on orchestral conductors. To consider his career move into conducting as 'allowing Berlioz to play out a metaphorical victory of composer-conductor over performer' is to overlook the impossibility of performing complex orchestral music adequately without someone taking command.[2] Such music continues to give aesthetic pleasure, entertainment, emotional satisfaction, and so on, to large numbers of people worldwide, and to provide employment to expert musicians following their long years of disciplined practice. If conductors are not always saints they are, at worst, a necessary evil; at best, they allow us to experience such works of orchestral magic as *Symphonie fantastique* to the full.

Diverse approaches to musical works can and should be allowed to coexist; considering Berlioz as a citizen of empire (at his birth and in his final years) need not exclude consideration of him as a provider of melody, harmony, rhythm, and colour partly for their own sake and partly for what they may suggest to the listener, with or without an explicit programme.

In *Music and Fantasy in the Age of Berlioz*, Francesca Brittan views Berlioz's output less speculatively, and with a wider perspective, as if through a larger, unblemished window. This is helped by including discussion of other composers of 'the age of Berlioz' and beyond. She considers how his often poor health affected Berlioz's states of mind, and not least the concept of the 'fantastic'.[3] A wide-ranging chapter, 'The *Fantastique moderne*', locates the musical *fantastique* within a wider framework of literature (especially Hoffmann), the visual arts, philosophy, and politics. The roots of such fantasy emerged before Berlioz's birth. His response seems unsurprising in a composer 'strongly attracted to romantic metaphysics, modern science, and revolutionary activism'. She has three chapters on the 'episode in an artist's life' (the symphony and *Lélio*), which first investigate literary tales (*Contes fantastiques*), some of which evoke visions of an ideal beloved. She proceeds to Berlioz's pathology, as revealed in letters to his closest confidants in the period leading to composition of the symphony: his sufferings in love for Smithson (usually referred to as Ophelia), his 'nervous exaltation', and a combination of physical and mental pain (Berlioz had remained in touch with some fellow medical students and teachers).[4]

Brittan moves to a discussion of early nineteenth-century writings on monomania, identifying symptoms like those Berlioz saw in himself, such as being haunted by a melody with a particular association. She notes that Berlioz's fixation 'was relatively benign, but, according to contemporary medical theory, it could lead to more dangerous forms of fixation, including the violent "homicidal mania"' (it was only after completing the symphony that Berlioz, then in Rome, seriously contemplated murder and suicide). The discussion continues with 'Doubled Selves' in art and literature, especially tales by Nodier, one of which has a character with an 'aural-erotic fixation'. For Brittan (citing the agonized letter to his father quoted in Chapter 1), Berlioz's '"other" self was not simply the product of lunacy but of self-scrutiny; it was the essential spiritual half of a genius self '.[5]

Brittan's chapter headed 'Grammatical Imaginaries' reaches music by detailing some ferocious early criticisms of Berlioz, and makes comparisons with other rebels against convention such as Victor Hugo. The earliest identifications of Berlioz's flaws mostly appear quaint in the light of musical developments since then, but some touch negatively on points that, viewed sympathetically or positively, might be considered his distinctive virtues. Contemporary lexicons and grammar books were the background to attempts to formulate a musical grammar. One such was by Berlioz's counterpoint teacher Antoine Reicha, who discussed melodic syntax in a treatise, with a strong predisposition towards symmetry.[6] Views of 'correct' melodic phrasing were still widely accepted, and Berlioz was indeed prone to ignore them, usually to good effect. The *Grammaire musicale* by Georges Kastner dates from 1837; Brittan suggests that his references to 'errors of rhythm' could have been 'aimed in part at Berlioz'. This is possible, but Kastner and Berlioz were on friendly terms, at least by 1839 when Berlioz wrote to him on 9 September soon after completing the immense score of *Roméo et Juliette*: 'No more notes to write. Amen, amen, amissimen!!!'; Berlioz later presented the autograph score to Kastner.[7] Brittan's chapter continues with a discussion of Berlioz's own writings and of his inclusive musical grammar or 'Fantastic Syntax' which, it is hoped, has been reflected on the pages of this book. Brittan makes other salient points, including the suggestion that the revolutionary and romantic manner of Berlioz (and Hugo) was perceived as a threat to social order.

Reading Berlioz within the artistic and political contexts of his time naturally favours *Symphonie fantastique* as the musical embodiment of the revolutionary spirit of 1830. Yet Berlioz was generally in favour of an ordered society, and was by no means opposed to monarchy or empire. His correspondence of 1848–51 make clear that he had no desire for a republic or for 'universal' (i.e. male) suffrage. Hugo, too, opposed the most radical elements of the revolution that broke out in 1848, when Berlioz was marooned in London and began writing his memoirs. They open with a lamentation on the state of his native land; the Preface is dated 22 March 1848. He later welcomed Louis Napoleon's coup d'état, not much admiring the man but welcoming the restoration of authority in the Second Empire and hoping for a restoration of the favour he had enjoyed from the Orléans monarchy.

Although Berlioz accepted distinctions such as membership of the Institut de France and the Légion d'honneur, he always remained artistically original, and in that respect was never 'part of the establishment'. His works of mixed genre opened new regions for others to explore (see Chapter 9), and his five-act opera *Les Troyens* is an epic rather than an imitation of the historically based *grand opéra* to which it bears a superficial resemblance. His last full-length work, *Béatrice et Bénédict*, is an *opéra comique*, but far from being a conventional one.

And the Programme?

The debate about music's relation to things outside itself – for instance, a play, a narrative, or a programme specific to an individual work – may never reach a conclusion. The wide-ranging treatment of programme music by Jonathan Kregor makes clear that Berlioz's excursions in overtures and symphonies are part of a general trend in this period, even the whole nineteenth century, although it is one which had roots in earlier music. In this Berlioz joined predecessors and contemporaries such as Beethoven, Weber, Mendelssohn, and Schumann.[8]

Whatever the motivations of other composers who wrote titled sonatas, overtures, or symphonies without publishing detailed programmes, Berlioz seems to have felt in the case of *Symphonie fantastique* that he could not afford to leave the audience's reactions to chance. But he did not repeat the experiment, unless we count the sung programme of *Roméo et Juliette* and the heading of its sixth movement (twenty-seven words in the original concert programme), to which Berlioz added a note in the published score. This movement, 'Romeo at the Tomb of the Capulets', so closely follows the dramatic action that he suggests in the note that it should be omitted unless the audience knows the play well, with David Garrick's version which Berlioz chose to represent, rather than Shakespeare's original ending.[9]

Leonard B. Meyer ended his *Emotion and Meaning in Music* by referring to programmes. Unlike in real life, in music:

in the absence of a specific referential framework, there is no causal nexus between successive connotations or moods .... There is no logical reason, either musical or extramusical, for any particular succession of connotations or moods. ... Although a program does serve to *specify* connotation, its main function is not to designate mood or *arouse* connotation. Music can as a rule accomplish this more effectively than a program can.[10]

Although programmes can indeed establish a 'causal connection' between 'moods and connotations', Meyer concludes by noting a drawback: the 'powerful temptation toward extramusical diversion'. This certainly applies to readings and misreadings of Berlioz's intentions, but perhaps we should ask ourselves whether these five movements would seem less like members of a single body, a symphony, if there were no programme to explain their sequence. Donald Tovey, in a note that dates from *c.*1903, took this view: 'his programme is here a very considerable help to the understanding of his music, and no analysis, nor any score, however miniature, should omit it'.[11] The same injunction applies to concert programme notes and notes published with recordings of *Symphonie fantastique*.

A less sympathetic view comes from a once widely read music historian. In discussing Beethoven, Paul Henry Lang sought to distance him from his admirer: the *Pastoral* 'is not program music in the realistic sense of Berlioz, for program music begins where the construction is directed by extramusical, whether literary or other, forces. The *Pastoral Symphony* is a true classic symphony'.[12]*Symphonie fantastique* is not named but is surely intended, although it is hardly clear how its programme could be considered 'realistic'.

Meyer's justification for programmes echoes Berlioz's comparison to the spoken dialogue of *opéra comique*, which explains the arias or other musical numbers that follow. But this symphonic programme can also be justified in musical ways: it explains the recurrences of the *idée fixe* in every movement and the intrusion of the bells and the *Dies irae* in the last; it explains rapid shifts of mood between reveries and passionate outbursts in the first and third movements, and the grotesque and fantastical character of the fourth and fifth; it accounts for the inclusion of a modern dance type (waltz), with the movement's residue of the ternary design of the traditional minuet.

Franz Brendel, Schumann's successor on the *Neue Zeitschrift für Musik*, took a different view about programmes from his predecessor when discussing Liszt's symphonic poems. What in the music seems strange, or even not to make sense (although making sense in music is a disputable concept) may be 'legitimised not by technical harmonic analysis, but by the *subject directly*'.[13] Perhaps unprejudiced technical analysis can also be called upon to assist comprehension, as musical details and the programme reflect each other. And there was a more mundane reason for having a programme; as Wotton put it, 'Berlioz, who, amongst his other accomplishments, had the makings of an excellent press-agent, wanted to interest the world, musical or otherwise, in the forthcoming performance of his work, and the bare announcement of "Symphony in C" would not have aroused the idlest curiosity in the Parisians of 1830.'[14] Before 1830 Berlioz had already contributed to a number of journals (in Berlin as well as Paris); for most of his career he earned more from publishing words than performing and publishing music. With no official position in Parisian musical life and having often to meet the expenses of performance himself, he can hardly be blamed for using his connections with the press to arouse interest in his music.

Some of Berlioz's defenders, despite Brendel, have tried to diminish the importance of the programme, claiming that he was happy to offer the audience only movement titles. Nicholas Temperley has effectively undermined their arguments.[15] And even if the programme was partly intended to arouse public interest, Berlioz meant it seriously; otherwise he would not have provided the symphony with a sequel. His active sense of humour is only lightly concealed in the symphony and emerges in parts of the *mélologue*. Perhaps because he wanted to end the first movement quietly, he added 'religious consolation' to the protagonist's sufferings. As the coda to the March, the only movement completed before the symphony's conception, he added the *idée fixe* and the gratuitously literal 'depiction' of the bouncing severed head. As for the finale's parodies, even for the professionals in the know, he would surely expect us to react appropriately, with a smile at least; satire without humour is a blunt weapon.

Some elements are not imaginary, but literal autobiography is not in question. An unbeliever well before 1830, Berlioz is not known to have sought religious consolation; he never met his beloved at a ball; he imagined, rather than actually dreaming, what appears in the final two movements. Certainly he experienced the *vague des passions* and *mal de l'isolement* (spleen), and he knew of the medical uses of opium. He was aware that an intended overdose might be too weak to kill him, but there is no reason to suppose that he attempted suicide before devising the programme. In 1833 he confided to Humbert Ferrand that such an attempt had been part of his courtship of Harriet Smithson, but he had prudently equipped himself with an antidote.[16]

Still less would it have been possible to compose such a work under the direct influence of any drug. So it is strange indeed, even naïve, to assert that Berlioz 'musically conveyed the effects of opium', from which one might infer that he transferred these effects to his audiences.[17] It is most unlikely that this effect would be identified through the music alone. As Berlioz put it when refuting a claim (in the dedicatory preface to Gluck's

Alceste) that the overture could convey the 'subject' of the opera: 'Musical expression cannot go that far'.[18] The subject of an opera is made clear by words; so it is with the programme symphony.

***

I have little sympathy for the view that *Symphonie fantastique* in some way overshadows Berlioz's later work, but it may indeed be his most radical step in opening what, in connection with Brahms, Schumann was to call 'Neue Bahnen' ('new paths'). Recent productions of his operas and other large-scale works provide a counterbalance to that view, and by now critics and musicians have mostly followed an often enthusiastic international public and come round to Berlioz. He had plenty of supporters in his own time. His conservatively minded German friend Ferdinand Hiller wrote an eighty-page tribute in his own memoirs.[19] Younger French composers could hardly escape his influence even if favouring genres (piano music, concertos, chamber music) to which Berlioz contributed little or nothing. Some took a different view of symphonic form, with engaging results; after Gounod and Bizet, Saint-Saëns and Franck both wrote untitled symphonies and programme music. What most of these later composers had in common with Berlioz is an attraction to opera, in which some of them – including Massenet, for whom Berlioz spoke up in the judgement for the Prix de Rome – were considerably more successful than Berlioz in their lifetimes.[20]

There were reasons for Berlioz to dramatize the symphony, including a lack of operatic commissions in the 1820s and after the initial failure of *Benvenuto Cellini* in 1838–9, but this only partially accounts for *Symphonie fantastique*, *Roméo et Juliette*, and *La Damnation de Faust*. Even if such works, and others, have been considered hybrid, even 'impure', and consequently excluded from the 'canon of masterpieces', it is worth recalling that Berlioz's resistance to rigid genre separation inspired others to stretch their imaginations and eschew mere routine, all the better if they found ways of their own to do it.

As for the 'canon' of the European tradition, it was founded on the alleged hegemony, in reality much exaggerated, of music by

German and Austrian composers, which for the nineteenth century runs the gamut from Beethoven to Brahms and used to be represented as 'mainstream'. In part-reaction comes criticism of the excessive emphasis on the 'work concept', although nothing can prevent, for instance, each Beethoven or Brahms symphony, or each of Berlioz's, from being separate works of marked individuality. In Berlioz's lifetime 'mainstream' would have been understood quite differently, as centred on opera – primarily Italian and, a little behind it, French. Even in Paris there was an Italian theatre, for a time directed by Rossini himself, and in Britain French and German operas were routinely performed in Italian translation, including Weber's *Der Freischütz* and Berlioz's *Benvenuto Cellini* (which despite its Italian setting was hissed off the London stage in 1853 by an Italian cabal).[21] Berlioz aspired to join the independent French wing of operatic tradition, but also applied for the job of directing at the Italian theatre; briefly employed to conduct in London (1847–8), he directed two operas by Donizetti, and in Paris he arranged mixed programmes in which his own music, and sometimes Beethoven's, was heard alongside music by Italians from Palestrina to Verdi.[22]

Criticism of the 'canon' concept is fair in that the repertoire of music performed and recorded is subject to change; there should be no barrier to the accepted masterpieces being joined by others. Conversely, however, criticism of the 'canon' is unfair if it means that new or rediscovered works should *displace* works that have survived the test of time, like Mozart's operas or Beethoven's symphonies; their distinction is unaltered by new music, or by the unearthing of fine music previously buried in libraries. The present popularity of Vivaldi's concertos does not diminish the excellence of Bach's; resurrecting symphonies by Méhul, Farrenc, Bizet, or Saint-Saëns – to name only French composers – does nothing to diminish the quality and originality of those by Berlioz, Franck, and Roussel. And this originality, a quality which few if any have denied to Berlioz, is a large part of the enduring fascination of his work: for musicians (including conductors), for music historians and analysts, even for the critical fraternity of which he was a distinguished member, and most importantly, for the attentive listener.

Notes

1. Inge van Rij, *The Other Worlds of Hector Berlioz: Travels with the Orchestra* (Cambridge: Cambridge University Press, 2015), 127–60; cited, 141–2, 145–52, 159.
2. David Curran, review of Inge van Rij, *The Other Worlds of Hector Berlioz, Berlioz Society Bulletin* 216 (August 2022), 43–7.
3. Brittan, cited, 41, 65, 71, 87.
4. See Peter Bloom, 'Berlioz's "Year of Medical Studies"', *Berlioz Society Bulletin* 214, 11–24, 215, 43–54.
5. Letter of 19 February 1830. *CG* Vol. 1, 309–13; Brittan, *Music and Fantasy*, 65.
6. Reicha, *Traité de Mélodie* (1814); Brittan, *Music and Fantasy*, 150–2.
7. *CG*, Vol. II, 576; presentation to Kastner, NBE 18, 365.
8. Jonathan Kregor, *Program Music* (Cambridge: Cambridge University Press, 2015); on *Symphonie fantastique*, 70–6.
9. See Julian Rushton, *Berlioz:Roméo et Juliette* (Cambridge: Cambridge University Press, 1994), 52–6.
10. Leonard B. Meyer, *Emotion and Meaning in Music* (Chicago: University of Chicago Press,1956), 271–2. My emphasis.
11. Donald Francis Tovey, *Symphonies and Other Orchestral Works*, reprinted from *Essays in Musical Analysis* (Oxford: Oxford University Press, 1981), 166.
12. Paul Henry Lang, *Music in Western Civilization* (London: Dent, 1942), 764.
13. Franz Brendel, 'F. Liszts symphonische Dichtungen', *Neue Zeitschrift für Musik* 49 (1858), 122, cited from Alexander Wilfing, 'Meaning and Value in Romantic Musical Aesthetics' in Benedict Taylor (ed.), *The Cambridge Companion to Music and Romanticism* (Cambridge: Cambridge University Press, 2021), 192.
14. Tom S. Wotton, *Berlioz. Four Works*, 14.
15. Nicholas Temperley, 'The "Symphonie fantastique" and Its Program'; Alban Ramaut, 'Berlioz et ses livrets ou Berlioz et l'intention dramatique: de l'invention du programme', in *Hector Berlioz: Regards sur un dauphinois fantastique* (Publications de l'Université de Saint-Étienne, 2005), 109–34.
16. Letter to Ferrand, 30 August 1833. *CG* Vol. II, 111–12.
17. John Tresch, 'Music and Technology' in Taylor (ed.), *The Cambridge Companion to Music and Romanticism*, 115.
18. 'L'expression musicale ne saurait aller jusque-là'. Berlioz, *À travers chants*, 156; (ed. Guichard), 176–7.
19. Ferdinand Hiller, *Künstlerleben* ('Artists' Lives', 1880).
20. Jules Massenet, *Mes Souvenirs et autres écrits*, ed. Jean-Christophe Branger (Paris: Vrin, 2017), 73.

21. Gabriella Dideriksen, '*Benvenuto Cellini* and the Politics of Opera Production in Mid-Victorian London', in David Charlton and Katharine Ellis (eds.), *The Musical Voyager: Berlioz in Europe*, 44–65; Sarah Hibberd, 'Berlioz's Waterloo? *Benvenuto Cellini* in London', in the same, 66–79; Ian Rumbold, 'Berlioz and *Le Freyschütz*', in the same, 127–69.

22. See the repertoire list in D. Kern Holoman, *Berlioz* (London: Faber & Faber, 1989), 612–27.

SELECT BIBLIOGRAPHY

*Please note that where multiple sources from a primary source appear, these are in chronological order.

Music Sources

Symphonie fantastique

Berlioz, Hector. *Symphonie fantastique*. Facsimile of the autograph manuscript, with introduction by Hugh Macdonald (Kassel: Bärenreiter, 2017).
    Berlioz: Fantastic Symphony, ed. Edward T. Cone. Norton Critical Scores (New York: Norton, 1971).
    Symphonie fantastique, ed. Nicholas Temperley. New Berlioz Edition Vol. 16 (Kassel: Bärenreiter, 1972). (Miniature score by Edition Eulenburg 422.)

Other Music Sources

Berlioz, Hector. *Lélio, ou le Retour à la vie*, ed. Peter Bloom. New Berlioz Edition Vol. 7 (Kassel: Bärenreiter, 1992).

Books and Articles

Banks, Paul. 'Berlioz's "Marche au supplice" and *Les Francs-juges*: A Re-examination'. *The Musical Times* 130 (January 1989): 16–19.
    'Coherence and Diversity in the Symphonie Fantastique'. *19th-Century Music* 8 (Summer 1984): 37–43.
Barzun, Jacques. *Berlioz and the Romantic Century*, 2nd edition (New York: Columbia University Press, 1969).
Bent, Ian (ed.). *Music Analysis in the Nineteenth Century II: Hermeneutic Approaches* (Cambridge: Cambridge University Press, 1994).
Berger, Christian. *Phantastik als Konstruktion: Hector Berlioz' 'Symphonie fantastique'*. Kieler Schriften zur Musikwissenschaft Vol. xxvii (Kassel: Bärenreiter, 1983).
Berlioz, Hector. *Grand Traité d'instrumentation et d'orchestration modernes* (Paris: Schonenberger, 1843).

146

Select Bibliography

Berlioz's Orchestration Treatise: A Translation and Commentary, trans. and annotated Hugh Macdonald (Cambridge: Cambridge University Press, 2002).

Grand Traité, ed. Peter Bloom. New Berlioz Edition Vol. 24 (Kassel: Bärenreiter, 2003).

À travers chants. Études musicales, adorations, boutades et critiques (Paris: Michel Lévy frères, 1862).

Annotated edition, ed. Léon Guichard (Paris: Gründ, 1971).

Trans. Elizabeth Csicsery-Rónay as *The Art of Music and Other Essays* (Bloomington: Indiana University Press, 1994).

Mémoires d'Hector Berlioz, membre de l'Institut de France (Paris: Michel Lévy frères, 1870).

Berlioz, Hector. *Mémoires d'Hector Berlioz*, ed. Peter Bloom (Paris: Vrin, 2019).

The Memoirs of Hector Berlioz, trans. and ed. David Cairns, 2nd revised edition (New York: Knopf, 2002).

Berlioz, Hector. *Correspondance générale d'Hector Berlioz*, gen. ed. Pierre Citron, 8 vols. (Paris: Flammarion, 1972–95); Vol. I (ed. Citron, 1972); Vol. II (ed. Frédéric Robert, 1975); Vol. III (ed. Citron, 1978); Vol. V (ed. Hugh Macdonald, François Lesure, 1989); Vol. VI (ed. Macdonald, Lesure, 1995).

Nouvelles lettres de Berlioz, sa famille, ses contemperains:Hector Berlioz Correspondance générale, Vol. IX, ed. Peter Bloom, Joël-Marie Fauquet, Hugh Macdonald, and Cécile Reynaud (Paris: Actes Sud: Palazzetto Bru Zane, 2016).

Berlioz, Hector. *Berlioz on Music: Selected Criticism 1824–1837*, ed. Katherine Kolb, trans. Samuel N. Rosenberg (New York: Oxford University Press, 2015).

Critique musicale 1823–1863. Vols. 1 and 3 ed. H. Robert Cohen and Yves Gérard (Paris: Buchet, 1996; 2nd edition Chastel, 2001); Vol. 7 ed. Anne Bongrain and Marie-Hélène Coudroy-Saghaï (Paris: Société française de musicologie, 2013).

Beyls, Pascal. *Estelle Fornier, premier et dernier amour de Berlioz* (Grenoble: Pascal Beyls, 2003).

Bloom, Peter. 'Berlioz pendant l'année de la *Symphonie fantastique*'. In *Musique et Société: Hommages à Robert Wangermée*, ed. Henri Vanhulst and Malou Haine (Brussels: Université de Bruxelles, 1988), 93–112. Trans. as 'Berlioz in the Year of the Symphonie fantastique'. *Journal of Musicological Research* 9 (1989): 67–88; revised reprint in Peter Bloom, *Berlioz in Time: From Early Recognition to Lasting Renown*, Eastman Studies in Music (Rochester, NY: Rochester University Press, 2022), 1–25.

Bockholdt, Rudolf. *Berlioz Studien* (Tutzing: Schneider, 1979).

'Die idée fixe der Phantastischen Symphonie'. *Archiv für Musikwissenschaft* 30 (1973): 190–207.

Bonds, Mark Evan. *The Beethoven Syndrome: Hearing Music as Autobiography* (New York: Oxford University Press, 2020).

Select Bibliography

Boschot, Adolphe. *L'Histoire d'un romantique*, 3 vols. (Paris: Plon, 1906–13).

Braam, Gunther, and Arnold Jacobshagen (ed.). *Hector Berlioz in Deutschland: Texte und Dokumente zur deutschen Berlioz-Rezeption (1829–1843)* (Göttingen: Hainholz, 2002).

Brittan, Francesca. 'Berlioz and the Pathological Fantastic: Melancholy, Monomania, and Romantic Autobiography'. *19th-Century Music* 29.3 (2006): 211–36.

Music and Fantasy in the Age of Berlioz (Cambridge: Cambridge University Press, 2017).

Cairns, David. *Berlioz*. Vol. 1, *The Making of an Artist* (second revised edition, London: Allen Lane/The Penguin Press, 1999).

Berlioz. Vol. 2, *Servitude and Greatness* (London: Allen Lane/The Penguin Press, 1999).

Discovering Berlioz (London: Toccata Press, 2019).

Citron, Pierre, and Cécile Reynaud (ed.). *Dictionnaire Berlioz* (Paris: Fayard, 2003).

Cone, Edward T. *Berlioz: Fantastic Symphony* (Norton Critical Score). London: Chappell, 1971.

Cosso, Laura. *Strategie del fantastico: Berlioz et la cultura del romanticismo-francese* (Alessandria: Edizione dell'Orso, 2002).

Dahlhaus, Carl. *Nineteenth-Century Music*, trans. J. Bradford Robinson (Berkeley: University of California Press, 1989).

Del Mar, Norman. *Conducting Berlioz*, ed. Jonathan del Mar (Oxford: Clarendon Press, 1997).

Dömling, Wolfgang. 'Die Symphonie fantastique und Berlioz' Auffassung von Programmusik'. *Die Musikforschung* 28 (1975): 260–83.

Hector Berlioz: Symphonie fantastique, Meisterwerke der Musik 19 (Munich: Fink, 1985).

Hector Berlioz und seine Zeit (Laaber: Laaber-Verlag, 1986).

Fifield, Christopher. *The German Symphony between Beethoven and Brahms: The Fall and Rise of a Genre* (Farnham: Ashgate, 2015).

Holoman, D. Kern. *Berlioz* (London: Faber & Faber, 1989).

Catalogue of the Works of Hector Berlioz. New Berlioz Edition Vol. 25 (Kassel: Bärenreiter, 1987).

The Creative Process in the Autograph Musical Documents of Hector Berlioz, c.1818–1840 (Ann Arbor, MI: UMI Research Press, 1980).

The Société des Concerts du Conservatoire, 1828–1967 (Berkeley: University of California Press, 2004).

Horton, Julian (ed.). *The Cambridge Companion to the Symphony* (Cambridge: Cambridge University Press, 2013).

Ironside, Susan. 'Creative Developments of the "Mal d'Isolement" in Berlioz'. *Music and Letters* 59 (1978): 33–48.

Kolb, Katherine. 'Berlioz's *Othello*'. In David Charlton and Katharine Ellis (ed.), *The Musical Voyager: Berlioz in Europe*, Perspektiven der Opernforschung 14 (Frankfurt am Main: Peter Lang, 2007), 241–62.

Select Bibliography

'Shakespeare and the *Symphonie fantastique*'. *Berlioz Society Bulletin* 203 (September 2017): 30–42.

Kregor, Jonathan. *Program Music* (Cambridge: Cambridge University Press, 2015).

*Kursell, Julia. 'Hearing in the Music of Hector Berlioz'. In David Trippett and Benjamin Walton (ed.), *Nineteenth-Century Opera and the Scientific Imagination* (Cambridge: Cambridge University Press, 2019), 109–33.

Lu, Julia, and Alexandre Dratwicki (ed.). *Le Concours du prix de Rome de musique (1803–1968)* (Lyon: Symétrie: Centre de musique romantique française, 2011).

Macdonald, Hugh. *Berlioz*, The Master Musicians (London: Dent, 1982).

Berlioz Orchestral Music (London: BBC Publications, 1969).

'Berlioz and Schumann'. In *Beethoven's Century: Essays on Composers and Themes* (Rochester, NY: University of Rochester Press, 2008), 42–56.

'Berlioz's Lost *Roméo et Juliette*'. In Peter Bloom (ed.), *Berlioz: Scenes from the Life and Work* (Rochester, NY: University of Rochester Press, 2008), 125–37.

'Berlioz's *Messe solennelle*'. *19th-Century Music*, xvi (Spring 1993): 267–85.

'Berlioz's Orchestration: Human or Divine'. *The Musical Times* 110.1513 (March 1969): 255–8.

'Berlioz's Self-Borrowings'. *Proceedings of the Royal Musical Association* 92 (1965–6): 27–44.

Maus, Fred Everett. 'Intersubjectivity and Analysis: Schumann's Essay on the *Fantastic Symphony*'. In Ian Bent (ed.) *Music Theory in the Age of Romanticism* (Cambridge: Cambridge University Press, 1996), 125–38.

Monelle, Raymond. *The Musical Topic: Hunt, Military and Pastoral* (Bloomington: Indiana University Press, 2006).

Münch, Marc-Mathieu. 'Berlioz, l'effet de vie et la Symphonie fantastique'. In *Berlioz, encore et pour toujours . . .* (Arras: Actes du cycle Hector Berlioz, 2015), 41–66.

Raby, Peter. *'Fair Ophelia': The Life of Harriet Smithson Berlioz* (Cambridge: Cambridge University Press, 1982).

Ramaut, Alban. *Hector Berlioz: Compositeur romantique français* (Paris: Actes Sud, 1993).

Ramaut, Alban (ed.). *Hector Berlioz: Regards sur un dauphinois fantastique* (Saint-Étienne: Publications de l'Université de Saint-Étienne, 2005).

Ratner, Leonard G. *Romantic Music: Sound and Syntax* (New York: Schirmer, 1992).

Rodgers, Stephen. *Form, Program, and Metaphor in the Music of Berlioz* (Cambridge: Cambridge University Press, 2009).

Rosen, Charles. *The Romantic Generation* (London: Harper Collins, 1996).

Rosen, Charles and Henri Zerner. *Romanticism and Realism: The Mythology of Nineteenth-Century Art* (London: Faber and Faber, 1984).

Rushton, Julian. *The Music of Berlioz* (Oxford: Oxford University Press, 2001).

Select Bibliography

The Musical Language of Berlioz (Cambridge: Cambridge University Press, 1983).

Rushton, Julian (ed.). *The Cambridge Berlioz Encyclopedia* (Cambridge: Cambridge University Press, 2018).

Schacher, Thomas. *Idee und Erscheinungsform des Dramatischen bei Hector Berlioz*, Hamburger Beiträge zur Musikwissenschaft 33 (Hamburg: Verlag der Musikalienhandlung Karl Dieter Wagner, 1987).

Schumann, Robert. '"Aus dem Leben eines Künstlers": Phantastische Symphonie in 5 Abtheilungen von Hector Berlioz'. Revised version in *Gesammelte Schriften über Musik und Musiker* (Leipzig: Georg Wigands Verlag, 1854), 118–51. (Originally in *Neue Zeitschrift für Musik*, July–August 1835; translations in Ian Bent, *Music Analysis in the Nineteenth Century*, and Edward T. Cone, *Berlioz: Fantastic Symphony*.)

[Signed 'Panofka']. 'Ueber Berlioz und seine Compositionen'. *Neue Zeitschrift für Musik* 17 (27 February 1835): 67–9, 18 (3 March 1835): 71–2.

Temperley, Nicholas. 'The *Symphonie fantastique* and Its Program'. *The Musical Quarterly* lvii (1971): 593–608.

Tovey, Donald Francis. *Symphonies and Other Orchestral Works* (Oxford: Oxford University Press, 1981), 164–70, reprinted from Tovey's *Essays in Musical Analysis* (London: Oxford University Press, 1935–9).

Van Rij, Inge. *The Other Worlds of Hector Berlioz: Travels with the Orchestra* (Cambridge: Cambridge University Press, 2015).

Visentini, Olga. *Berlioz e il suo tempo*, 2 vols. (Lucca: Libreria Musicale Italiana, 2010).

Vogel, Oliver. *Der romantische Weg im Frühwerk von Hector Berlioz* (Stuttgart: Steiner, 2003).

Wotton, Tom S. *Berlioz: Four Works*, The Musical Pilgrim (London: Oxford University Press, 1929).

Websites

Association nationale Hector Berlioz: www.berlioz-anhb.com.

The Berlioz Society (London): www.theberliozsociety.org.uk.

The Hector Berlioz Website (founded by Monir Tayeb and Michel Austin, 1997): www.hberlioz.com/index.html.

Musée Berlioz (La Côte-Saint-André): www.musee-hector-berlioz.fr.

INDEX

Index

Index

Printed in the United States
by Baker & Taylor Publisher Services